Ladies' Tract Road Run

Compiled by Annie Chapman BEM to mark the 20th Anniversary of the Ladies' Tractor Road Run organised to raise funds for Breast Cancer Research through

In association with

The David Brown Tractor Club (Suffolk and Norfolk) Ltd

Ladies' Tractor Road Run

ISBN: 9781804674376
Perfect Bound

First published in 2023 by bookvault Publishing, Peterborough,
United Kingdom

An Environmentally friendly book printed and bound in England by
bookvault, powered by printondemand-worldwide

Acknowledgements

With enormous gratitude to Jane and Gareth Roderick-Jones for their unstinting help and enthusiasm in putting this book together. Without them this book would never have seen the light of day.

Thanks also to all our contributors for their writings, poems and photographs which make up this publication.

Our grateful thanks to our official photographer Jonathan Slack for his years of photographic memories some of which appear in this book. A full selection of photographs can be viewed on our website and facebook page.

www.ladiestractorroadrun.co.uk

©Jonathan Slack photographs reproduced by kind permission of Jonathan Slack

Our appreciation goes to each member of CRUK who has helped us in the last 20 years.

Thanks to Elaine Verhaag and the team at CopyDiss for their support in the design and editing of the book.

Note: Photographs are intended to reflect the spirit and atmosphere of the run and do not necessarily identify individual contributors

The Beginning

I've been searching for many weeks to find a way in to the story of The Ladies' Tractor Road Run. I came up with the idea that, just maybe, the way in is to start with the tractor! KBJ 666 has played a crucial part in this journey and has been the mascot for the Run since the beginning.

On 16th November 2021, my husband, John, and I delivered my trusty tractor into the hands of experienced restorers in north Norfolk. KBJ 666 is a 1950 David Brown Cropmaster purchased from a sale in Suffolk in 1986, the first time KBJ had been out of her original county, as we live in Norfolk. Referring to the log book which had luckily been retained, we discovered that KBJ had originally been owned by my late ex-father in law from Stradbroke. In the years following 1950, KBJ had been through various owners including a spell by the sea at a plant nursery in Walberswick where she was used to retrieve drift wood from the beach. Some doubtful restoration work has taken place over the years, some not respecting the fact that she had a galvanised undercoat. Now, all these years later, we felt that she deserved a facelift! The irony

of a David Brown of that era is, despite the paintwork appearing red, the colour is actually called 'Hunting Pink'. We collected KBJ gleaming and rejuvenated the week before the Run last year.

The idea for the run came one November evening when John and I sat by the woodburner mardling over what I might do following my imminent retirement. The discussion revolved round various charity ambitions which, frankly, were out of the question considering my age! Riding across deserts or mountains, even with an organised charity trip were really a little too far fetched. The idea for the ladies' road run came from John following our ramblings over the achievable efforts for charity we had already undertaken. Belonging, as we did then, to two tractor clubs, The Old Ram and The David Brown (Suffolk and Norfolk branch) we had already shared happy days with fellow members exploring unseen environs of these two counties from the double seat of KBJ. "Why don't you organise a tractor road run just for ladies?" suggested John. Why don't I! The spark of the idea soon grew and I found myself thinking how can I do this, who would come, where would we go, start, lunch, etc.etc. and WHY? Obviously it had to be a charity with ladies in mind. Recently a friend of ours had been diagnosed with breast cancer and this had taken everyone quite by surprise and the awareness of this disease and its prevalence in this country were quite an eye opener. It seemed the obvious choice.

So, we had the idea of the run and the charity, what next? Where do we start from? As Boundary Farm (our home) is a little remote and not easily accessible we decided we needed somewhere near home with parking for lorries/trailers etc. We approached our farming neighbour, Richard Cole, who kindly agreed we could use a piece of land on South Green, Pulham St. Mary. The tractor line up for the run was on an adjacent piece of land owned by the late Michael Griffin. As with most runs, a break of some sort was the usual format, so our Suffolk farmer friend, Roy Goodwin, agreed we could use a meadow at Syleham Hall. Having had a lifetime love of maps, it gave me great pleasure to pore over the OS map of this area to work out a possible route for our run. How far could we sensibly go, could we include some off road sections, where would we be safe away from main roads, roundabouts etc.? The proposed route took us through the villages of Rushall, Brockdish, over the river Waveney into Suffolk and into Syleham.

Basically, the first requirement was to see if anyone would be interested in taking part! I rang two friends, one the farmer's wife who had been diagnosed with breast cancer and the other a friend from the tractor world who was familiar with road runs. Both were enthusiastic and began thinking of friends who might do the run. I began to make a list of possible participants and also possible sponsors of a charity supporting breast cancer. Cancer Research UK was the obvious choice so I floated the idea past them and they were, of course, delighted to help! It seemed the idea 'had legs', so full of enthusiasm I approached our local bank, the then Midland, and spoke to the manager (we had such a thing in 2003!) and asked to open an account. 'How much did I think we might raise?' No idea! Possibly 4 or 5 thousand pounds – how long is a piece of string? OK, we were away.

Then came the question of advertising it! I designed a poster using a photograph of me on KBJ at the Henham Steam Rally the year it was held on the Royal Norfolk Showground. We had ascertained from the David Brown Tractor Club that the event would come under one of 12 annual events covered by their insurance. We had a starting place and a lunch place but no time had been established. It seemed reasonable to choose a date between hay and harvest to find a quiet time of the year for farming folk! We decided on the first Sunday in July and that date has remained ever since. We had the details, what, where, when and why we were doing it. We were fortunate to have sponsorship from a printing firm used by John's office. In the meantime I made a list of names and addresses of likely supporters, bought some stamps and envelopes for my first mail out! Posters and entry forms were the first exciting evidence that this idea of John's back in the previous winter was actually underway!

We had absolutely no idea how many entries we would get, but as soon as the first entry arrived in my post box there was a thrill of excitement that, at least, someone wanted to join me! The entries started to trickle in, the phone started ringing, "Annie, I hear you're doing a run for ladies only, please may I have an entry form?" and so it continued........That first year, bearing in mind it was going to be a 'one off', we were thrilled to have 50 pioneering ladies! Official CRUK sponsor forms had been issued to each lady with the challenge of raising as much money as possible for breast cancer research. I truly believe that one of the reasons for the success of this event has been the charity. Everyone knows someone who has had it, is suffering from it or who has sadly been lost to it.

Ladies had been advised that the lunch break would be a picnic that could be shared with family and friends at the venue of Syleham Hall where we had plenty of meadow space for both tractors and for parking cars. Taken quite by surprise at lunch time we had our first taste of wet weather! A sudden downpour had us reaching for our wet weather gear! Thankfully it dried up pretty quickly and we drove back in sunshine. Advice has since been offered every year about being prepared for all eventualities regarding the weather. Not everyone takes this on board! On our return to the meadow on South Green, my middle daughter, Libby, a keen amateur photographer, called everyone together for a group photograph, now known as 'The Pioneers'! It is displayed in our barn along with the photographs of every Run we have done since.

The Pioneers

The elation felt by that first group of ladies was palpable, so many smiling faces, some very relieved to have even got round! "You must do it again Annie!" echoed through the group. Needless to say, we did it again and again and again! These pioneering ladies were rewarded for their fundraising efforts by the knowledge that they had raised £16,500! Each of them had raised their own sponsorship recorded on an official CRUK form, cash or cheques being the method of payment in those days, (life was so much more simple then) my estimate of 4 or 5 thousand being blown away!

Another precedent was set that year; we had a Reunion and Presentation Evening here at Boundary Farm, two months after the Run. Our barn was cleared, cleaned and decorated with pink for the presentation of the cheque to our local representative from CRUK who at that time was Beverley Mottram-Smith. We were supplied with some pink tee-shirts for a special photograph for their publicity. We still have a video of that Run taken by the late Janet Keeble from the Harleston Tyres van part of our support group. We are so grateful to the Keeble family who have been an essential part of our back up team for every Run since, with daughter Meryl also becoming a Pink Lady. What a stunning first!

In our second year we decided to start from a stubble field near our house giving us a bit more space. A wonderful turn out of 70 tractors was recorded by a BBC TV crew with Amelia Reynolds who came to 'cut the tape' at the start. One of the memorable things for me was having to dismount from KBJ to record an interview with her, there being no suppressor on my tractor it was interfering with their technical equipment. That year the skies were very threatening as we grouped for the traditional photograph, only realising the next day how lucky we had been not to get seriously wet. Part of the field was underwater with a lake the size of a tennis court with ducks swimming on it. The joys of outdoor events in England!

Another aspect

An aspect of the Run which has been totally unexpected has been the involvement of the general public. Their enthusiasm and participation have extended beyond cheering us on our journey through the villages. Even at the first Run I was surprised to see so many people come to see us off. This mainly included family members keen to see their daughter, sister, mother or friend take part in this unique event. Since then it seems to have developed into a much loved spectator sport! Over the years we have witnessed private parties in people's gardens, everyone dressed in pink, toasting us with pink drinks, cheering us on our way. We've had picnic tables at the side of the road with candelabra, hedges adorned with pink bras, signs written to welcome us and an old boy sitting in his driveway on his vintage tractor. One year we had a whole group of children from the local village waving pink flags they had made at school! Entering our town of Harleston we've had the punters in the local pub garden raising a glass in our honour. The list goes on.

Harleston town itself is transformed during the summer with bunting to celebrate the annual town Festival. Much credit must go to Carol Wiles, MBE who, with her team, contribute to the provision of bunting for the town and the shops. Carol also organises the team of collectors with the charity buckets both in the town and

surrounding villages for our run. I do have to apply to South Norfolk Council each year for a licence to collect money. After the run I have to submit the name of each collector and how much money was in each of their sealed buckets. Laborious but very rewarding.

Many of the shops, especially the charity shops, decorate their windows in pink with model tractors, flowers, cards, ribbons etc. Distributed throughout the town are about 30 flags on poles above the shops and businesses depicting my tractor and the words 'Pink Ladies', made especially for us by a resident and sponsored by a local business. These town flags are constantly changed throughout the year to support many local, national and even international events. It is one of the specialities of this town and the people in it. It is very humbling to see the effort which so many people make in support of The Run. All of this decoration, made by the people, is supported by the people from the town, the villages and many holidaymakers who fill our town on the day with their endless clapping, cheering, smiles and tears, from start to finish of our trip through the town. There are many ladies who have spoken to me after the Run who express total surprise, not only at the number of people there, but their own emotion felt, faces set with smiles at the joy of the welcome and tears of sheer emotion at the underlying reason for our being there. I don't think any of my ladies have driven through Harleston without tears in their eyes or pouring down their smiling faces, or a large lump in their throat. It is almost indescribable. The atmosphere is electric and even having done this Run for so many years, it never fails to choke me up.

We had a complete change of venue in 2006 thanks to the kindness of the Woodrow family at Topcroft. We had the privilege of the use of the grass runway of their private airfield. An unexpected spin off from this venue was meeting Maurice Hammond, a talented aviation engineer and pilot who kept his Mustang in the adjacent hangar and who subsequently took some stunning aerial photos of the Run. For some years Maurice gave us a stunning 'flyby' at Gawdy Hall and at Thorpe Abbotts Airfield flying low above our heads, sensational! The weather was amazing and our first experience of really high temperatures, 33 degrees. This really brought home to me the need for ladies to be protected from extreme weather, many of them having no sun cream, hats or water. This recommendation is now written in the comprehensive notes that are sent

out to all entrants each year. We had a lovely run using some off road areas round Denton, Alburgh and Redenhall and again using the beautiful meadow at Gawdy Hall for the lunch break.

In total contrast, the following year, 2007, was a different ball game. It poured with rain for days and days beforehand and even on the morning of the Run it was horizontal rain! Thankfully, having regular contact with David Green, then the Managing Director of Gawdy Hall Estate, he assured me that it would stop raining by mid morning. He, of course, was quite right. The downside of the days of rain was that the runway at the airfield was under water! This was a complete nightmare as far as we were concerned. Thankfully, in those days, farms still had areas of 'set aside' and the Woodrow family kindly allowed us an area at the back of the farm for parking the tractors. Unfortunately we had to ban all public vehicles and arrange for all the lorries and trailers to be parked on hard standing around the farm buildings. If I remember correctly, I had already mailed out to all the participating ladies that we would have to reroute the run to exclude all the off road sections. No problem for tractors but the amount of mud we would have carted onto the roads was a problem we couldn't cope with. Needless to say, everyone cooperated with a good grace. It was that experience of our susceptibility to the vagaries of the British weather that prompted a need to find a starting point on hard standing. And so, on to our next chapter of the Run.

A few miles down the road from us is the Thorpe Abbotts Airfield, a private airstrip, part of an old USAF base from World War 2 and part of the farm belonging to Sir Rupert Mann Bt. John wrote to Sir Rupert explaining our event and our dilemma. After a site meeting with him and subject to some very reasonable conditions he agreed we could use the runway in 2008 and we haven't looked back since. Adjacent to the airstrip is the Museum of the 100th Bomb Group which has allowed us separate access for the public away from the tractors, a real benefit on safety grounds. Sir Rupert also requested respect for his crops and bird life on his farm and also required fire extinguishers to be on hand and no dogs allowed on site. These conditions are still a requirement and respected. We also send Sir Rupert copies of a comprehensive Risk Assessment, produced by John each year, the Insurance documents and copies of all correspondence that has been sent to all entrants including the safety check document, the notes about the day, the itinerary and the route map. Copies of all these documents are distributed to the Managing Director at Gawdy Hall, the local Police in Harleston, senior marshals and the area representative from Cancer Research UK.

It has been a great boon for us to have this facility just a few miles from home and has meant control of gates and keys has been so easy with the curator of the Museum, Ron Batley, the retired farm foreman. All the volunteer staff at the Museum have been great supporters and ambassadors for the Road Run. Here we are, all these years later and nothing has changed. The reassurance of all their support is so much appreciated. Apart from 2020 during the first year of the pandemic when we had to cancel the usual Run we have been back at Thorpe Abbotts ever since. Another advantage of the venue has been access to local villages in south Norfolk and north Suffolk which gave us an easy approach to Harleston. Apart from the slightly gut churning Shotford Hill, the route is very popular and is adhered to every year. We have had every conceivable weather condition since we've been at Thorpe Abbotts but thankfully, the concrete runway has stood us in good stead.

Despite some serious wet weather over the years, the other asset we have really enjoyed is the beautiful parkland and meadow at Gawdy Hall. Always reassured by David Green, the hay has always been cut before the Run, although one wet year we had to run on cut hay, thankfully for us it was very thin. The land there is very forgiving and drains very freely. In 2015 having endured torrential rain all morning, by lunchtime it stopped raining and the sun came out bringing back the smiles to some very wet ladies! My biggest memory from that occasion were the two words echoing round the huge meadow at Gawdy Hall, 'wet knickers!' This was a common experience for many ladies who hadn't understood the meaning of 'proper waterproof clothing'. They do now! They all have their own stories to tell.

Due to the increase in numbers of tractors we have extended the lunch break from one and a half hours to two hours. We found that by the time the last tractor had arrived it was nearly time to leave! This has allowed for a much more relaxed time. We have always encouraged the 'Picnic Lunch' to be shared with family and friends and have always invited any pu to 'bring your own picnic' and come along and j us and view all the lined up tractors. We have alw avoided commercial food wagons, the only concess being a local ice cream van and the only facili supplied are the loos! Over the years this picnic grown, hundreds of people turning up to support Pink Ladies. Whole families have reunions on that day in July. Having gained confidence in the first of the run, the ladies now experience some glori off road tracks through the 2000 acres of Gawdy H It is such a privilege to have access to a beautif managed farm in such a productive county. We h witnessed the changing crop rotations includ wheat, sugar beet, peas, beans and oil seed rape. will be eternally grateful to Sir Rupert, David Gr and the owners of Gawdy Hall for their kindness cooperation in supporting our event.

Spinoffs!

There have been many spinoffs from this event result in some wonderful experiences for me personally always on behalf of the Pink Ladies.

The first award I received was totally unexpec In 2008, Paul Fleet, who was our local CR representative at that time, had put my name forw for 'The Flame of Hope Award'. This award was gi to the National Fundraiser of the Year at a ceremo in London. Not being aware that the LTRR had ma such a huge impression at CRUK, I was comple taken by surprise when he announced that I had w Another great honour at the dinner was to sit nex the CRUK Chairman who, at that time, was Da Newbigging.

A lovely, unusual event happened in 2007 when Ro Connah (our chief marshal) and his wife Anne, F White (our chief mechanic) accompanied John myself across the Fens to Ely Cathedral for the Prem of a special piece of music written and conducted John Rutter. This lovely piece, entitled 'Look to Day', was written especially for Cancer Research U What a great honour for all of them from a top cl composer and The Eye Bach Choir. John and I ha played at our wedding while we signed the register!

The Olympic Torch.

In 2011 CRUK put my name forward (as a volunteer fundraiser for them) to the Olympic Torch Committee for the 2012 Olympics the following year. I was flattered to be nominated and thought no more about it as it was so far in the future, and why me? Anyway, 3 months later I was shortlisted! Another 3 months later I was selected, subject to the usual checks, and 3 months after that I started my training! The requirement was to carry the torch for three hundred metres, preferably running or jogging, not walking. At that time, age 70, I could not have run to our front gate! So began a 3 month journey of fitness training. My daughter, Julia, lent me a wonderful book called 'Run Fat Bitch Run'! Basically it was a kick up the proverbial to get out from under your duvet and start moving. If anyone had told me at the beginning of those 12 weeks that I could jog 3 miles I wouldn't have believed them - I could and I did - a great feeling! As I only had to jog 300 metres I was glad of the fitness as it turned out my section of the route was uphill. Many of the lovely family which is the 'Pink Ladies' turned out

to support me in Aldeburgh in Suffolk on a glorious day of sunshine and cheers! What a huge honour and one I value highly. By chance that day we met the courageous Rachel Lane. A tribute to Rachel is written by John in the story section of this book.

In 2012, South Norfolk Council very kindly presented me with a new award, 'Queen's Diamond Jubilee Community Award', for Community Fundraiser of the Year'. Our local BBC senior news presenter, Stuart White, presented me with the award, again, one earned by the group not just me.

A couple of years later I was greatly honoured to have The British Empire Medal (Civil Division) conferred on me by Her Majesty The Queen for my services to the community. One of our Club members had put my name forward and I was delighted to receive my medal from the Lord Lieutenant of Norfolk, Richard Jewson, at a small formal ceremony at The Great Hospital in Norwich with John and my three daughters in attendance. It was an interesting event hearing the stories of other recipients' achievements. I always feel it such a pity that I can't share a piece of these honours with all the Pink Ladies, it really is a joint effort.

Much more recently my little red tractor graced our television screens with an appearance on ITV's Pride of Britain Award. I was so fortunate to be nominated locally and although I didn't get through to the final what great unexpected publicity for the Ladies' Tractor Road Run!

CarFest!

Early one Monday morning the day after the Run in 2017, I had just got out of the shower when my phone rang – 8.20am!? It was the producer from the Chris Evans Breakfast Show on Radio 2. Chris had seen a photograph in a national newspaper that morning of ladies in pink on tractors driving through our local market town of Harleston. His interest aroused, he put out a request on the radio that if anyone knew what it was all about to phone in. A lorry driver from this area heard the request, contacted a friend of his, a Pink Lady, and it was suggested that Chris should contact me. Hence the call from the producer, 'would I be prepared to talk to Chris live on the radio?' No problem – they'd call me back in 20 minutes. I was getting ready to go to my ballet class and seriously wondered if it would actually happen. It did, they rang back and I had about a 5 minute chat with Chris about the Road Run, his tractor and the possibility of his wife driving in the Run etc. etc. He finished up inviting me and any other Pink Ladies to take tractors down to CarFest South at Jody Scheckter's place in Hampshire that August Bank Holiday. Someone would be in touch.

Anyway, eventually, after what was weeks later and much nail biting about details of numbers, insurance, camping, passes etc. etc. we went. In the end we had 6 decorated tractors at the amazing event. Glorious weather, family camping, great musical acts and a huge Sunday morning Carnival and a big kiss for me from Chris Evans! It was a wonderful experience to have been part of. The Red Arrows graced the skies and a stunning weekend was had by all. The commitment was, and is, demanding for anyone going with a tractor. Obviously it's a long way down to Hampshire and we had to be there by Thursday night for 4 nights as we weren't allowed to leave before Monday morning. No problem in 2017. We were honoured to be invited back the following year, and in fact in subsequent

years, but the experience in the second year was completely different from the first year as it cou have been!! Torrential rain, gale force winds, flood tents, wet clothes with no way of drying anything! haven't been back since, but a small stalwart group Pink Ladies has been back each year flying the flag the Pink Ladies and Cancer Research UK. We do make any money from the event as it raises funds Children in Need but it raises the awareness of bre cancer and the diverse use of vintage tractors. Tha you Chris Evans!

In 2017 the East of England Co-op took over Budge Supermarket in Harleston which was closed for to refurbishment. Some months later I and my frie Carol Wiles MBE, were very honoured to open t new Co-op Store along with my tractor. Ironical some months later Carol and I were asked to op the new convenience store of Budgens at Lawrenc Garage on London Road! KBJ has been in attendan at many other functions including CRUK Race for Li and Pretty Muddy on the Royal Norfolk Showgroun The 10k course included a 'tractor pull' where sm teams of ladies were required to pull the tractor abo 20 metres between some cones. Great fun and anoth example of 'flying the flag' for breast cancer.

2017 delivered its final surprise when, in October, Jo and I received a letter from the then Prime Minist Theresa May, saying that she had given us a 'Poir of Light' award. It was, and still is, an award made I the P.M. on every weekday of the year to voluntee who are judged to have made a real difference in th communities. We felt quite undeserving as we'd nev heard of the award, but pleased, of course, that the Pi Ladies were well and truly on the national stage!

Many other events have been enjoyed by myself wi KBJ 666, many other road runs with the David Brow Club and The Old Ram Tractor Club. We have bee regular attendees at The Grand Henham Steam Ral over many years and have been pleased to have ha other pink ladies in attendance. There has alwa been a mention of the Pink Ladies' Tractor Run durir the parade round the Grand Ring, flying the flag on again for Cancer Research UK. In September 202 I was invited to take KBJ to Strumpshaw Stea Museum for their Annual Autumn Event along wi another decorated tractor supplied by a couple of loc ladies who had done the run a few years previousl

The visitors on the two days were invited to make a donation for the programme of the weekend events. We were so grateful for the generous donations given by the public and totally bowled over by the generosity of the owner of the museum. Thank you one and all for a really lovely event!

Over the years I have delivered many talks to many different groups including, women's groups, farmers' clubs, Probus, Rotary and the Women's Institute. A few years ago I was invited to talk to Sandringham W.I., sadly, but probably thankfully, HM The Queen wasn't in attendance! I was also pleased to take my Olympic torch to a couple of local primary schools much to the delight of the pupils. They were able to have their photos taken holding the torch, copies being sold to the parents with the money being shared by the school and the Pink Ladies. All the clubs have been generous with their donations to the cause.

Christmas trees aren't something you would easily connect with tractors and pink ladies. Years ago a local church at Dickleburgh staged a colourful Christmas Tree Festival open to everyone. I don't think pink was a colour normally associated with Christmas but our entry was very pink and glittery! All pink ladies were invited to decorate an old type of clothes peg just as they wished. We had some stunning creations in the style of fairies, angels and even tractors, pink being the most popular choice of colour. Every year we put in an entry varying the decorations each time and being delighted to win a small monetary prize for our charity. The last year it was held we were so excited to win the 1st Prize, a great honour as the judging was by public vote. Sadly, like so many other voluntary events, the enthusiasm and support diminished and it is no longer held.

One of our stories written by Roger Connah, our chief marshal, details his experience of one of our days out to the CRUK Institute at Addenbrooke's Hospital in Cambridge. I have been privileged to have taken some coach loads of supporters to view the extensive research work undertaken there. We were treated to a light lunch followed by an enlightening talk by one of their scientists on various aspects of breast cancer. Our eyes were truly opened by the tour of their extensive laboratories with explanations of the priceless pieces of technical equipment used by world class scientists. We quickly realised how valuable was our contribution

of funding to help in some way towards the cost of all this research. Unfortunately, due partly to cost and Covid, these visits are no longer available. What a great insight into how much CRUK value the contribution made by the Pink Ladies. Everyone there knows who we are!

Along with local events, John and I have had the pleasure of attending some unique experiences in London. These have included invitations from CRUK to special occasions. One event in London included meeting Princess Alexandra who told us of her memory of driving a tractor during the war! There have been two memorable visits to Buckingham Palace Garden Parties, one held shortly after my back operation when I had to take my own collapsible chair and had to go through a special security check! The other involved a tour of the gardens and a viewing of a selection of Her Majesty's specially adapted Landrovers! Other trips included a Christmas service at St Pauls Cathedral and a special Women's Day Ladies Lunch at Park Lane.

A very moving event I was invited to speak at was an International Women's Day at Swainsthorpe Church. There were many heartfelt stories from ladies with, sometimes disturbing experiences in other walks of life. It was a real eye opener into a different world and one that has stayed with me and made me appreciate how lucky I am in my life.

None of this would have happened or continued without 'the wind beneath my wings', my husband John. It was his idea and just wouldn't have got off the ground without his input. All correspondence that leaves this house is checked by John for content, relevance and spelling! Each year since 2004 we have had up to 8 of our tractors participating in the Run. This entails everything from checking each one for road worthiness, tyres, steering, batteries, brakes etc. and that's just the tractors! Each one of these tractors has been driven by a lady, most of them with limited experience, if any, of driving a vintage or classic tractor. I've lost count of the number of ladies John has taught to drive, always with consummate patience, thoroughness and humour. Many of them have returned year after year, some just come for one year for the experience. It is such a rewarding thing for him to have done in respect of raising people's awareness of driving a tractor and also of the thousands of pounds they have raised over the last 20 years!

Apart from the tractors, John has spent many hours maintaining all the road signs including the David Brown Tractor Club signs which are put in place at 7 o'clock on the Sunday morning of the Run with the assistance of our chief marshal, Roger Connah. These signs, if put out the day before, have a habit of being altered or disappearing! The large direction signs to the venue at Thorpe Abbotts and Gawdy Hall are put in place on the Saturday with help from Rob White, our chief mechanic and Gareth Gaunt, our senior lorry parking marshal. They also take all our electric fencing posts from our paddock to Gawdy Hall. These are used to divide the meadow for tractors to be parked separately from the general public for the picnic. The 'office' caravan also has to be transported up to the airfield ready for the early start on Sunday morning.

Needless to say, at the end of the day on Sunday, after all the ladies, tractors, lorries, supporters etc have gone home, the reverse of setting up has to be undertaken! All of this is achieved with the help of our aforementioned team! This also includes litter picking at the airfield and Gawdy Hall. Fortunately this is [not] an onerous task, bins having been supplied by Jo[hn] there is very little litter at either place, mostly pink [?] having blown off the tractors. People have been m[ost] respectful at both of these venues for which we [are] very grateful.

I have often compared this whole event to a theatr[ical] production. John and the team of marshals are v[ery] much the set builders and the back stage crew, Jo[hn] being the stage manager, not always noticed what th[ey] do, but the show would never go on without the[m]. Another part of this crew are Keith Broomhall w[ith] his set of six loos on a special trailer, and, now sad[ly] the late Rick Barnes who transported loos kindly [lent] by the Norfolk Ploughing Society. More on that fr[om] Keith in his own words in the 'stories' part of this bo[ok]. The 'props' department is most definitely the trac[tor] owners, usually husbands, dads, brothers and m[any] times just complete strangers who offer their tract[ors] to willing ladies. They teach the ladies to drive th[em]

2008 'Flame of Hope Award' with Chairman CRUK David Newbigging

safely, fuel them and very often transport them to the venue. We certainly couldn't do this without them!

Every event of this size is required to have first aid cover and we are grateful to have had the services of Tim and Tina Peck of ATP who cover us for both first aid and fire. They have been with us for years and are so much appreciated as are Harleston Tyres who have been with us from day one. In the beginning we were supported by Keith Keeble and his, now sadly, late wife Janet and subsequently one or other of their sons, Darryl or Joel. Not only are they there in case of tyre problems but also carry water and fuel, just in case! Their services have sometimes been required more for the latter than tyres!

Also included within the Run are two 4 x 4 vehicles with trailers in case of breakdown. Embarrassingly it was my tractor in 2015 which broke down, in pouring rain, having only gone a few miles! It was quite a serious problem which couldn't be fixed there and then so I had to abandon it to the tender care of Chris Thomas and ride with my daughter Libby. Fortunately Libby always follows behind me on the run driving a Super Cropmaster belonging to Rob White, chief marshal. Cropmasters have double seats which legitimately allowed me to be a passenger. Passing through Harleston, I think the crowd thought I was a passenger because I had recently had serious back surgery, until they realised the tractor coming through the town on a trailer was mine!

Keeping a pictorial record of the event are Jono Slack and Walter Pipe. Jono very kindly set up our website many years ago and continues to photograph all the ladies from various stages around the route. Hundreds of photographs from many runs are available to view on the website. His photographs have featured on the poster for very many years, this 20th Anniversary Year being no exception. Walter produces a DVD each year, the income from which he donates to the charity. Previews of the DVD are shown at the Presentation Evening in September and available to order.

In recent years we have had added media and press coverage from Kate Royall, our volunteer press officer who has worked hard in promoting the run in the local press, local and National magazines and radio. It's been a pleasure to have had the opportunity to speak on our local radio stations who are always very supportive in getting the word out there!

Neighbouring farmer, Martin Everett, has always been kind enough to position a large farm trailer on part of the runway at Thorpe Abbotts for the group photograph taken at the finish of the Run. He also houses my little KBJ 666 overnight in one of his barns prior to the Run.

The Front of House volunteers are my helpers in the caravan who check in all the entrants with a smile, a programme and a rosette. These rosettes I introduced, I think in 2006, as a memento and a thank you to the ladies, many of whom use them each year to decorate their tractors or themselves! The programme contains the names of all the entrants, the make, model and registration number of their tractor and thanks to the whole team of volunteers who make the event happen.

The ladies are each given a ribboned medal from Cancer Research UK in recognition of their achievement. I would like to thank all the Cancer Research UK representatives with whom I have had the pleasure of working over the last 20 years, a wonderful team of dedicated charity workers.

Also included are thanks to all the landowners to whom we are truly indebted over the last 20 years!

The cast, The Stars of the Show are, of course, The Pink Ladies!

I'm always impressed by the many diverse ideas implemented by some ladies to raise sponsorship. These have included cake stalls, quizzes, bingo nights, a fashion show, garden, meadow and allotment sales, dog shows, raffles, coffee mornings, sweepstakes, and family mini road runs! Already planned for this year is another Fashion Show and another Dog Show, always popular!

What started off as a straightforward way of collecting sponsorship money has finished up, in my eyes, rather more complicated! Cash and cheques were the order of the day, each being easily recorded and accounted for. Over the years, with the introduction of online banking and payment options, it has become more of a challenge. I am very grateful to my daughter, Libby, for her understanding of and dealing with the technical side of sponsorship. Ladies are now able to set up their own page directly with CRUK which means that all monies paid in online go straight to the LTRR account at CRUK, plus any gift aid where applicable. Ladies still have the option of cash or cheques and there are many of them that still use that option. Libby has set up a spreadsheet enabling her to account for all monies received by whichever means! I'm very relieved to have this knowledgeable help.

Libby has also, annually, prepared certificates for all entrants using a photograph of them on their tractor, thanking them for joining us. In the beginning we sent individual photos but over the years this became impossible so a group photo, courtesy of Jono Slack, has been used on the certificate. In 2021 we were unable to have a group photograph because of Covid restrictions so a lovely image of my tractor taken by Libby and the CRUK and David Brown Club logos were used.

In the strange year of 2020, because of tight Covid restrictions, we were unable to hold the run at all in the usual place or manner. As restrictions were gradually lifted, we were allowed groups of up to 30. So, I arranged a mini Run from here called the Boundary Farm Breakout on the 13th September with 30 local ladies on tractors and a loyal team of socially distanced marshals! A wonderful day was enjoyed by all, in glorious sunshine and free of tight restrictions. This freedom was short lived as the following day we were once again restricted to groups of only 6! Despite no advertising at all and driving half the usual route in reverse, we were amazed how many people turned out to cheer us on our way. There was a great feeling of community everyone so pleased to get out in the sunshine, all socially distanced and delighted that we were able to at last have a go! There were no public street collections of any sort so all moneys we received were placed in collecting goblets in various shops in town or sent directly to me, or done online. Our team of ladies and marshals were delighted to receive a CRUK

tea towel printed with a group photo of the socially distanced ladies! There were other small groups of ladies who organised their own mini runs that year and with other various fundraising enterprises we managed to raise £28,000. Unbelievable!

There are only two other groups of tractor ladies that I know of: The Lincolnshire ladies who followed our lead and started a Run in 2010 and one in Australia! The original Boston group organisers came to see John and myself to discuss the basics involved in starting a run. John and I were thrilled to attend their inaugural just north of Boston in Lincolnshire. I'm pleased to say their run is still taking place, done through the David Brown Tractor Club and for the same charity. In Australia, thanks to modern technology called the internet, an interested party picked up on our idea and started their own small group of tractor ladies. They raise money for a different charity and wear purple but what a great tribute to the Pink Ladies! 'Sisters are doing it for themselves'!

Dedication.

I would like to dedicate this book to all my Pink Ladies, with special thoughts for those we have sadly lost along the way.

Annie

The Boundary Farm Breakout (Covid year)

John

If you asked me on a bad day I might say I still love my wife despite the LTRR. But, most days, I would tell you that I still love my wife partly because of the LTRR. Annie and I have been married to each other twice so we know all about testing the strength of a relationship. The LTRR has given us the chance to work in partnership for 20 years and has enriched our lives through the many special people we have met, worked with and sometimes lost.

When we first conceived the idea of a ladies' tractor road run I have to make the appalling male confession that boobs were the first thing that flashed into my mind when we talked about which charity we should support. Apart from one long lost relative on my late father's side there was no history of breast cancer in my family or Annie's, so it was just chance or fate that brought us to this cause. And fate has been kind to us as that cause has generated a 'brand' that, if we could sell it, would be worth a fortune. I can think of many people, from nurses in Norfolk to investment bankers in central London, who follow the fortunes of the LTRR every year.

Because I was a lawyer it was automatically assumed that I would deal with all the tedious stuff like insurance and risk assessments. They may be tedious but they're not half as stressful as having to get tractors ready for the Run, including Annie's of course. Ask anyone who does vintage or classic tractors (actually anything with an internal combustion engine) and they will tell you that they behave perfectly until you put them in the public eye. They are devious, cunning beasts, always devising new ways of catching you out. Even Annie's tractor, which receives endless tlc , has broken down, once just after the beginning of the run and once within half a mile of the finish!

The wise men will gather round and say ''Thass gotta be fuel or electrics''. Well of course it has – there isn't anything else that will stop an engine running apart from total seizure which is usually an unmissable diagnosis! In one case our electrical fault was actually the very rare occurrence of the teeth stripping from the bevel gear which drives the distributor from the camshaft. Devious, cunning and hugely expensive having had to get a new one made with the help of computer aided design.

If the tractors are a challenge, their prospective lady drivers are something else! After 20 years of tuition I can tell within 5 minutes whether I have a natural, a willing learner, a challenge or (very rarely!) someone beyond training. To the great credit of all the ladies I have trained, I have never had a cross word with any of them and they are invariably doing their best to make me happy. Their safety and the structural integrity of my tractors are paramount so I do not give up easily. The pay off for me is the smiling face and the pure joy of the lady who has completed her first road run and experienced the unique experience of seeing crowds turn out to support her.

We have been asked a million times ''What's your secret?'' ''How does it work?'' I could write pages on why I think it works but the truth is I don't really know. Our first run in 2004 raised what was, in those days, an incredible £16,500 from 50 tractors. It was a concept that exploded like a volcano, a local happening turning into an annual national and even international event. Hardly a month goes by now when we don't get a cheque from someone who has raised money for the Pink Ladies: a quiz night, a wedding anniversary, a wake, a birthday party. Just this month (Dec. '22) a cheque arrived from friends who had scrapped a caravan and sold the bits for us.

The LTRR is promoted by the David Brown Tractor Club (Suffolk and Norfolk) Ltd of which I have been chairman for many years. The Club generously gives us a free hand with the organisation of the event, although many members contribute as marshals or tractor owners. Outside the club I have the invaluable support of two dear friends: Roger Connah, our chief marshal and Rob White, our chief mechanic. They have been with us from the beginning and I know I can completely trust them to deal with any problem or difficulty in the right way, as well as being prepared to do all the menial stuff such as putting up signs and barriers before the run and litter picking when it's all over.

Ask me what is my most profound memory of the LTRR and I would immediately say July 2012 when Annie carried the Olympic Torch for Cancer Research UK, not just because of her achievement but because of a chance meeting on the beach afterwards. Rachel

Lane was resting after walking her section of the route. Suffering from terminal secondary breast cancer she was supposed to do her stint in a wheelchair but had the grit to get up and walk. Rachel was a very special young lady and we were delighted when she agreed to come and present the 2012 cheque at the Reunion at our home in September of that year. She passed away a few weeks later. I will never forget talking to her as she sat in her brother's car before the presentation, on oxygen and worrying that she would not cope with what we had asked her to do. She did. Magnificently. ''If it were not for you I would not be here'' are Rachel's words of hope that will stay with me for ever.

John Chapman

Annie with daughters Libby, Julia and Catherine, 10th Anniversary 2013

String Vests & Dry Socks

As memories fade and the years begin to merge into one another, certain images remain as clear as the day they happened. In 2006, on my second Pink Ladies Run, we were on a rural stretch of road near Alburgh, on one of the old routes. Without warning, a figure leapt out of the hedge in front of my tractor. All I recall seeing was a string vest, a pair of cargo shorts and a can of Newcastle Brown. "Good on yer, gal!" yelled the figure, before disappearing once more into the hedge.

Jane Roderick-Jones and dogs

A few hundred yards further on, there was a fine looking traditional farmhouse, with a table and chair set out at the entrance, complete with silver ice-bucket and champagne flute. A distinguished looking lady sat at the table, politely clapping and repeating "Well done! Well done!"

Over the years the number of people turning out to cheer us on has increased dramatically. In remote corners of the countryside, there are impromptu picnics in field entrances, full-blown lunch tables set out in gardens with parasols and cake stands, driveway barbecues, and everywhere, pink banners, dogs dressed in pink, and people waving and clapping and wishing us well.

Every run has been an intensely emotional affair, and people taking part often talk about the fabulous reception we always get as we pass through Harleston, and now also Pulham and Brockdish. Few of us manage to get through these communities without shedding a quiet tear or two. We are grateful to all the people who turn out to cheer us on along our route, the generous shopkeepers and the volunteers collecting money from the crowds, and of course the marshals and helpers, and Keith with the loo trailer. I would also like to mention all the people who make such an effort to encourage us outside their houses along the route. For me, it is a delight to see the bunting, and picnic tables and barbecues and dogs in pink collars (this is the only time I enjoy seeing animals dressed up!) in the middle of nowhere. A small effort, perhaps, but to us it makes a very big difference.

Of course, sometimes it rains. I recall one year when we were so drenched by the time we reached Gawdy Hall for the traditional lunchtime meet-up with friends and family that the only thing that kept me going was the arrival of my best friend Sue, with dry socks and trainers and a steaming Thermos flask.

I have seen some changes over the years. Nowadays, the costumes and tractor decorations have become a lot more flamboyant. It has become a tradition in my household to hold a tractor decorating party on the day before the run, when a group of friends arrive with ribbons and pompoms and poppies and tinsel and I hand over the tractor and let them loose on it (stipulating only that any modifications should be reversible). The dogs get to do a dress rehearsal in pink and red bow ties and have their photos taken too.

I started taking part in the Pink Ladies Road Run in 2005, when I heard of an opportunity to drive a borrowed tractor, and collect some money for a worthwhile charity at the same time. And, of course, the sheer fun of taking the Brockdish ford as fast as possible! I had had a great fondness for tractors, particularly old and lived-in tractors, since I was a teenager doing summer work in the fields, but had had little chance to keep my hand in over the years. I loved that first run, and decided I would definitely take part the next year and the next …

Taking part in the runs I found out more about Cancer Research UK and particularly the Breast Cancer appeal. I was, and still am, impressed by the fact that apart from administration costs, every penny of the sponsorship money goes to Cancer Research UK. I also found out more about the incredible passion, and care, and commitment, of everyone involved in the charity, from the individual fundraisers to the scientific staff to the frontline medical practitioners. Countless lives have been saved already by money raised to support Cancer Research, but there is still a huge amount still to be done, as all around us people are still having to battle against cancer, and all too often they are losing the fight. I was hooked!

But 2022 was an especially poignant run for me, as I had to say goodbye to my best friend Sue, supplier of dry footwear, yet another victim of breast cancer. I made the run in Sue's honour, to celebrate her life and to mark our loss as she succumbed to the disease. She was an extraordinary person who was more active, more adventurous, and more cheerful and positive with cancer than most of us manage to be when we are fit and well. She kept up the fight against wave after wave of cancer for over thirteen years, until finally it proved too destructive for even Sue to manage.

Several years ago she bought a house in Shelfanger but she disliked the original name of the house, so she renamed it The Poppies, for the simple reason that she liked poppies. She put up some poppy curtains, and then she put up some decorative poppies outside the house, and finally she went out and commissioned some metal poppies which still adorn the gates of the house to this day. The usual roses which had been used to decorate my tractor were replaced this time with poppies in Sue's memory. I found myself inundated with donated poppies, some of them from a church in Newcastle. Hopefully they won't be missed, at least not until Remembrance. A favourite decoration was a poppy painting by my friend Florence, aged 10, which thankfully survived the run.

A special moment for me was when I turned in to Gawdy Hall meadow and was greeted by my dog Royce, and his brother Jack, who lived with Sue until she became too ill to look after him – yes, both wearing pink collars.

I would also like to give a special mention to the very trusting owner of the Massey Ferguson I drive. Richard unhesitatingly lets me drive off on his tractor, fuelled up and serviced – and also thanks to all the other generous tractor owners who make it possible for those of us who don't have our own tractors to take part in this wonderful event.

So thank you, Annie and John, and everyone else involved in the Pink Ladies' Tractor Run, whose imagination and hard work have led to this moment, once again: the annual donation of funds to Cancer Research, to help them in their constant search for ways to fight this most widespread and terrible disease.

Jane

The Pink Ladies Ride Again

Pink Ladies, the time has come
For the 17th Annual Tractor Run.
A hundred tractors, maybe more,
Ask Annie Chapman, she's keeping score.
Thorpe Abbotts Airfield marks the start,
thank Sir Rupert Mann for where we park.
Raising money is the name of the game,
on pretty tractors, not one the same.

Breast Cancer Research is our plan,
grabbing sponsors where we can.
For us, this cause has special meaning,
so check your breasts and go for screening.
Pink, pink, pink and just more pink,
we're all here to make you think:
Of lives that are lost and lives still to live,
the way to help – please can you give?

Wigs galore, amazing clothes,
tractors dressed with flowers and bows.
A sturdy bra and sensible shoes,
if you're driving, stay off the booze.
Ladies, please do make a note,
remember sun-cream and a coat.
Rain or shine, we're not quitters,
but no-one likes soggy knickers!

Jono's here to take my picture,
thank goodness he's a regular fixture.
Running round to different places,
for photos of our smiling faces.
Making memories, waving poses,
sunburnt arms and shiny noses.
From start to finish he's on the hop,
Brockdish ford a favourite spot.

Supporters come to line the street,
clapping hands and stamping feet.
The crowds that help us on our way,
make for an emotional day.
Look, there's Carol, Mrs Harleston,
collecting funds, with a yellow sash on.
Spot tractor flags with Annie's face,
as we trundle on through Market Place.

By kind permission of Gawdy Hall,
come see us one and all.
Bring a picnic for your lunch,
have you ever seen such a happy bunch?
Count all the tractors if you can,
and watch out for the ice-cream van.
A lunch time breather, a chance to rest,
then we're off, the next bit's best.

Through private tracks our homeward drive,
makes you glad to be alive.
Along bumpy lanes we pick our way,
past fields of corn that gently sway.
It really is a privilege
to see what lurks behind the hedge.
Fantastic views not seen by car,
really special, how lucky we are.

Back at the airfield, tractors away,
a final photo to end the day.
Rosettes and medals handed out,
to those who helped, a final shout.
Thanks to our marshals, tractor lenders,
rescue crews and tractor menders.
For our Pink Ladies give a cheer,
we hope to see you all next year!

Libby

Behind the Scenes

As regular participants in local tractor runs, it came as no big surprise when Mummy (Annie) and my stepfather John said they were thinking of doing their own run, but just for ladies. The chosen charity was a complete no-brainer with far too many friends affected by breast cancer in some way or another.

I hadn't driven a tractor since leaving my father's farm in '84, and as a photographer and taking pictures was more my thing, I said I'd grab my camera and come along. Meeting in a small field near the top of Garlic Street, 50 tractors lined up for the off. There were a few worried faces as tractor owners relinquished their tractors to the ladies (followed by ill-disguised relief when they were returned unharmed at the end of the day). Grabbing a few rolls of film, I found a sunny spot on the route near Brockdish which gave a lovely view of the tractors making their way down the road to pass me for a quick photo. With only 36 shots on a roll, it was the fastest film change I have ever had to do. The group shot of 'The Pioneers' was a spur of the moment thing, and then the shout went up to do it all again the following year. The rest I suppose is this history.

Mummy and I then had great fun trying to match faces to names as each lady participant was sent a mounted photo with their certificate. With no numberplates on the front of the tractors, it was quite a task. We all felt very proud of the £16,500 raised that year.

In 2005, I again found a suitable vantage point off-road along the beautiful tracks of the Gawdy Hall Estate and the group photo at the end was a slightly more organised affair. I was offered the use of a large trailer to stand on to get a better view of the gathered group. I was then rather embarrassed as they all struck up 'happy birthday'; there was nowhere to hide. We were lucky with the weather that year, as driving past the field a couple of days later there were ducks swimming where we had been parked.

Both the ladies and their tractors were starting to sport a bit more pink, the outfits becoming more and more outrageous but touchingly interspersed with yellow sashes quoting 'I'm a Survivor'. The decorating of tractors has now become an art form with some showing real flare. We always advise a quick check round to make sure all moving parts are avoided, and not forgetting the risk of a hot exhaust pipe. Ribbons, balloons, flags, flowers and teddies are common sights but the poignant 'in memory of' signs bring home the real reason we keep coming back each year.

I say we, as in 2006 I suggested that Mummy should find another photographer – I just had to find a tractor and take part. I was incredibly fortunate that John's friend, and our chief backup mechanic, Rob White had a David Brown Super Cropmaster which he offered to lend me. With both of us squeezed into the double seat – it was designed for smaller bums than mine – we set off around the roads and tracks of Thompson to take her for a test drive. Stopping to change gears and ratios was a bit of a challenge at first but I was soon declared safe. Rob has kindly offered her every year since, for which I'm very grateful. The double seat has been very useful, especially in the year that Mummy's tractor decided that 2 miles was enough for one day. She rode with me for the rest of the run.

The weather at the beginning of July is always unpredictable and we've had everything thrown at us. In 2006 my first run started from Topcroft airfield, we were scorched; sunscreen and water the top priority. The following year, we weren't able to use the grass runway as it was under water! Despite the beautiful location at Topcroft, it was a relief when Sir Rupert Mann kindly agreed to the use Thorpe Abbotts airfield with its acres of hard standing.

Taking part in the run is very much the icing on a much bigger cake. Driving through the Waveney Valley is a huge pleasure, as much as it is a challenge on a 70-year-old tractor. A sturdy pair of boots and an even sturdier bra are my go-to essentials, before even considering the vagaries of the British summer. My pink bag always contains a drink, sunscreen, tissues, towel, phone, scissors, and a full set of waterproofs whatever the forecast! New, and returning ladies, have been very quick to learn that coming unprepared leaves you somewhat vulnerable: from sunburn to soggy knickers, we've seen it all.

Preparation is everything. There is so much that goes on behind the scenes before the day. Before the entry forms are even printed, there are posters, letters, notifications and permissions to sort. Mummy's dining room table rarely sees the light of day as it's covered with tractor run paperwork for most of the year.

For me, the anticipation is already building when I arrive at the airfield on the morning of the run, leading a convoy of tractors to take our places in the line-up each year. It's just a sea of pink and the line of over 100 tractors is quite remarkable. John, with his trusty Land Rover, leads off towards Brockdish where there's always a huge turnout to watch as we cross the ford. A quick wave to Jono Slack – taking the first of a series of photographs of each tractor throughout the day. Up through Syleham and on to Weybread, the views across the valley are spectacular. Having used the same route for several years now, it seems there is support around every corner. There are messages of thanks and hope, garden parties, bras in hedges, and bunting everywhere.

A brief halt by the hockey club, to make sure we're all together, before climbing Shotford Hill into town. I'm lucky enough to have my family join me for lunch and there's always loads of chocolate birthday cake (much to Rob's delight). A giant picnic in a beautiful meadow at Gawdy Hall with hundreds of like-minded friends is a chance to reflect on the journey so far, and wipe away the tears from the increasingly emotional support that overwhelms you driving through Harleston.

Heading off after lunch takes us off-road, back towards Pulham St Mary. It all seems much calmer, till the roar form the crowd at Pennoyers lifts you all the way to the end.

The (now well organised) group photo marks the end of the day – for some of us, and the few shout-outs given at the time cannot convey the thanks we feel. There are so many people without whom this run just wouldn't function. It is not just the ladies who take part, but the army of volunteers behind them. It would be impossible to name them all or even realise that some of them are there. Mummy and John have organised everything for the day, preparing tractors and checking the route. Fire safety and first aid are covered, as well as mechanics, breakdown recovery, and tyre fitters, not to mention the excellent toilet facilities. From the ladies at the check-in caravan to parking, there is one of Roger's team of marshals for everything, including every junction along the route. I've probably missed out someone but each and every contribution to the day makes it such a wonderful way to raise funds for the Cancer Research UK Breast Cancer Fund. There are ladies who go out of their way to fundraise throughout the year to boost their sponsorship. There is Carol's team of ladies who rattle buckets along the route and schoolchildren who donate their pocket money. Others help in other ways, giving their time or expertise. Friends and families fill our sponsor forms or donate online, and to be within reach of raising £1 million is testament to all of them.

My small contribution starts after the run, with an enormous spreadsheet. Mummy and I counting cash from collecting buckets, collating the sponsor money, checking the sponsor forms and online donations. I design and print all the certificates in preparation for the reunion party in September. It's a great way to end the year with everybody involved joining together to celebrate what we have achieved while watching Walter's DVD of the day, and hopefully handing over an enormous cheque.

It seems we all know someone whose life has been changed by cancer. We're just trying to do our bit to help.

Libby

My Pink Ladies Tractor Journey

My first Pink Ladies' Tractor journey started in 2012 when I borrowed my friend Janine's tractor. I wanted to help raise money for this good cause as I had lost both my parents and many dear friends to cancer and to raise awareness and money for the charity, while having fun on a tractor dressed in pink seemed perfect.

I was totally blown away by the support of everyone who lined the route and driving through Harleston Town was just amazing and brought tears to my eyes and has done for the last 10 years I have taken part. Every year I'm still blown away by the support for Annie's Pink Ladies' Tractor Run. We have had beautiful hot sunshine and torrential rain (that's a year I won't forget) over the years but each and every run brings smiles and waving whatever the weather.

Now to raise a few extra pounds without asking the same family and friends each year, my lovely friend Jo and I decided over several gins that we would do a Bake Sale; now anyone that knows us would think we Are super organised but that is not the case! Jo and I organised everything via WhatsApp, no meetings, and sitting round a table drinking gin. So with the local church booked we sent out messages via social media asking for cakes to be baked and all our family, friends and local businesses did us proud and we raised a good amount.

This spurred us on to think of holding another event and in true Jo & Jayne style via WhatsApp we organised a Dog Show, not sure if it would even take place due to the pandemic. But in July 2021 we held our first fun dog show and again the support from everyone was just incredible and we raised money for the Pink Ladies while having lots of fun. As I type this today we are planning this year's events via messages again, maybe another dog show or a quiz, who knows, but there will be a J&J event.

So many people make this such a fabulous day: Annie, the ladies on their tractors, the marshals who are incredible, the crew with their collection buckets, the support crew, the people that loan their tractors to us, and everyone that lines the route.

I am very proud and humbled to be a part of this Tractor Run and have met some incredible ladies along the way, and formed some wonderful friendships. I hope I will be able to take part for many years to come, and with all the money raised hopefully a cure can be found one day.

Jayne

Raised as a City Girl

Raised as a city girl in a London Borough, driving a tractor was never on the radar! However, meeting the love of my life, from East Anglia, my life took a very different turn in my mid 30's, and I ended up blissfully married, living in Suffolk and owning a horse.

Life has had its challenges, but meeting, and sometimes unfortunately losing, some incredible, caring, loving and selfless people has inspired me to be grateful and not take a moment for granted. So, when my husband, myself and by now four horses moved to Norfolk, I was incredibly lucky to meet yet two more very special people, who have once again made my life richer for knowing them.

So, in September 2018, who'd have thought, when a friend and I took two of my horses out riding along a country lane to explore the local area around our new home, that this would lead to a chance meeting with a lovely lady who stopped to admire the horses and end up with me, dressed in pink, driving a tractor which was also dressed in pink?

This lovely lady was thrilled to have more "horsey" company in the neighbourhood, as was I (us horsey people like to stick together and talk of little else but horses, although it now includes tractors!) as she had two of her own at home. As clichéd as it is, the rest, as they say, is history. A wonderful friendship was formed

with Annie and her incredibly cheeky yet very patient husband, John (yes, he had to teach this city girl to drive a tractor!)

So, within five months of moving to Norfolk, meeting Annie and John, I was signed up to dress in pink, decorate a tractor in pink and drive it around some country roads In Norfolk, to raise money for a very worthy charity, CRUK. I never saw that coming!

My first was in July 2019. I borrowed a tractor from John, who I quickly named Phoebe (why not?!) and met yet more incredible, inspirational and fantastically fun people. Yes, it's true her décor was inspired by my love of horses, and she did manage to carry a pink plastic horse around on her bonnet for the entire trip, thanks mainly to my nutty, beautiful friend Zara, who tied it on so securely it took nearly an hour to get it off! The wonderful Frances took me under her wing on the day and made sure I remembered to enjoy it, as well as being utterly terrified that I'd damage John's vintage tractor, get lost or forget to take the handbrake off!

I was very generously sponsored and supported by my friends and family on the day. Zara handmade the decorations for the tractor and travelled from London to support me, as did my Mom and Aunt. My close friends Liz and Paula and their husbands met us at Gawdy Hall where we all had a picnic together and this

was all coordinated by my wonderful husband Nigel, whose gift of being totally unflappable, even when surrounded by hysterical, giggling women dressed in pink, did not go unnoticed. He's now joined the merry band of volunteers to help, but that's his story to tell!

I could barely eat I was so emotional, although those who know me will know that didn't last long. I'm always hungry! I couldn't believe the total raised by all the Pink Ladies and had a thoroughly fabulous day, with laughter, cheers, aching arm from waving and emotional tears as we drove though Harleston but all very firmly inside my sports bra! Thanks for the tip.

Then came "The Covid": let's not dwell, we all know everything was cancelled, including the 17th Annual Pink Ladies' Road Run. Life, for many, came to a crashing halt, but CRUK still needed our help because Covid, unfortunately, doesn't stop cancer.

When some restrictions were eased in August, I was extremely honoured to be asked to take part in an impromptu Pink Ladies' Road Run. On a much smaller scale (gatherings were still restricted), but no less pink! I borrowed the lovely Phoebe again and took part in the Boundary Farm Breakout. Sadly, due to the restrictions and the lack of time, Annie, John and the Team had to organise (it takes months and months of their hard work), this would be a much quieter affair, mostly off-road and back streets, no bunting or crowds and no street collections. How wrong were we!?? Hundreds of people were safely supporting us from their gardens, their cars and in the fields. Harleston, although the main Thoroughfare was closed, was more emotional than ever with many residents out cheering and yes, someone had even put up the bunting! A day I will never forget, a memory to cherish and an uplifting experience, not just because of my sports bra!

And so to 2021, life was beginning to open up again and the postponed 17th Annual Pink Ladies' Tractor Road Run could and did happen. By now I had my own tractor - I know, right? I named her Annabelle, Annie for short. Duly decorated, dressed up and thrilled to be one of the Pink Ladies again, we set off. The crowds were incredible, hundreds of people everywhere! And everyone, including us, cheering, clapping, crying, laughing; it was incredible and so very powerful to see and hear the human spirit released and full of joy, love and support for one another.

The support was enormous. It always means so much to us. But the support we received in 2021 surprised us all I think. The amount raised was astonishing. At a time when fundraising was curtailed, donations fell and lots of charities struggled, we managed to touch the hearts of all those who sponsored us and for that, I personally thank you all, you are truly making a difference. I can't wait for the next one!

Gail

My Story of Becoming a Pink Lady

I lived most of my life in Essex but when my husband George retired we moved to Harleston and I can tell you it was the best decision we had ever made. The minute I saw the town on a Sunday morning in October 1999, I fell in love with it. There was hardly anyone around but you just know when a place is right for you. Within a week we had found and agreed to buy our chalet bungalow which we moved into permanently when George retired in March 2002. We very quickly adjusted to country living and were amazed just how welcoming the town was and how lovely our neighbours were.

One July Sunday, probably about 2010, we were surprised by a huge number of people in the town. Obviously something was about to happen and very soon we knew. We were fascinated by large numbers of tractors magnificently decorated in pink raising money for breast cancer research. As soon as I saw them I was hooked as my mother had been treated and survived breast cancer in 1962 when I was still at school. Of course we were very keen to donate but I decided then that I would love to be one of the pink ladies. Being a townie, I had no way of getting a tractor to join them.

In 2014 my daughter and son in law, who had also fallen in love with the town and the area, decided to change their lives by moving to Norfolk. They moved onto a farm and loved to come and watch the pink ladies.

They were talking to the farmer about the fact that I would love to take part, and to my delight he said that I could use his 1959 Massey Ferguson tractor. My only problem was that although I have been driving since 1975, I have never even contemplated driving a tractor, so the first job was to learn. It was a very daunting prospect as I had no idea how different it was. I had forgotten what it was like to have no power steering and a smooth gear change. Luckily I managed to learn and to my delight on 3 July 2016 I took part in my first tractor run. I'm told that the smile never left my face and after a long and very exciting day I was buzzing! I then did another three runs but unfortunately in 2019 the tractor was deemed to be unroadworthy so I had a problem.

After a phone call to Annie to tell her I could no longer participate, within 30 minutes I had a call to say she had found a friend who was prepared to let me use his 1954 David Brown. The first time I drove it from his house and he followed me to check that his tractor would be in safe hands. He was happy so I was allowed to take it out on a couple more trial runs before the big day.

I have now completed six tractor runs and become good friends with the owner. The first year was the year of my 70th birthday and I promised myself then that I would continue until I was 80 at least! Hopefully I'll be doing it when we get to £1,000,000!

FOOTNOTE

My husband George, who sadly died in hospital in January 2021, was one of our greatest supporters. When I arrived home after the 2021 run it was to an empty house with no one there to share the happenings of the day, and although I was happy, it felt a little strange. As many of us do at the end of the run, I went straight to the kettle to make a cup of tea. As I sat down to drink it, I turned on the television and the first image that appeared on the screen was me. I knew Anglia News had been filming and talking to Annie and other ladies but not to me, so it was surreal.

Frances

Cupid

My story is a bit different to most people's, I'm sure. I had been on my own all my life, never having met the right man. I did the tractor run with my friend, Carol. She had just been through a divorce. I had been doing computer dating, but the people I had met were not my type. Some were very strange and I got to the point I didn't want to meet any more. I told Carol I was going to delete my profile off the website. Carol said to give it one more go, but this time to put on the photo of me on the tractor. She said she had more comments from her photo than anything else. She also said to log in as soon as I got back from work and to leave it on until I went to bed. She said that way the website would put me at the top of the list and show me as actively seeking someone. I did as Carol said and a week later Steve messaged me. The first line he wrote to me was: "You have a nice tractor but I wouldn't think you need all that extra pulling power!!" That was what sold me on Steve. We have been together ever since. He has brought a lot of happiness to my life and I don't know what I'd do without him. He was well worth waiting for.

You have not only helped people with cancer, but also been a Cupid!

Dawn

Pink Spectacle

In 2006, quite by chance, I met a lovely lady who was living in Essex at the time and now lives in Norfolk. We are almost identical in age, but our lives have followed very different paths. I have always lived in an urban environment and endured a career in the corporate world. By contrast she has enjoyed a rural existence with several roles about as far from corporate life as is possible. Despite this, our relationship has developed into a close and valuable friendship. During many visits to Norfolk, she has introduced me to a variety of experiences of country life. About eight years ago, I started to hear about the Pink Ladies' Tractor Run. There were stories and photographs and I provided limited support from afar through sponsorship. In the intervening years the encouragement to experience the even first-hand grew. Unfortunately, it has always clashed with a local community event which I am committed to.

In 2021, after making my apologies locally, I decided to head to Norfolk for the first weekend in July. As I live in Greater London, there is limited need for tractors, but I was confident that whilst experiencing the event I would be fully capable of shaking a collection bucket or marshalling traffic. But no … as soon as I had committed to the weekend, I found that I had been lined up with my very own tractor and I was heading for full immersion in the event. After a couple of lessons with my generous and patient tractor owner, I felt confident enough to think I could enjoy driving and most importantly be safe. I launched myself into planning my pink outfit and sourcing a selection of decorations for my trusty steed.

Fortunately, I have not suffered from breast cancer myself, nor did I participate in memory of any particular person, but we all know people, mainly women but also men, who have suffered from this horrible disease.

Research is essential to reduce the incidence and improve the prognosis of those who succumb. I set myself a reasonably ambitious target for fundraising and was blown away by the generosity of my family and friends, raising six times my initial target. The quirky nature of the event captured the imagination of so many people who exclaimed "What fun!" or "Well, that beats a 10km run!"

I didn't really know what to expect, but I had the most fabulous time. From attaching the first bow to my tractor to removing the last flower, and everything in between. Each tractor was unique, each person was unique, everyone's reason for taking part was personal and individual but collectively it made the most amazing pink spectacle. I had heard about the crowds in Harleston but the people in their gardens, those parked up in gateways and those on good humour who had inadvertently been caught up in the convoy of 100+ tractors all waving and cheering, were a pleasant surprise. Perhaps on the back of Covid-19 (although I suspect not) it was a real "feel-good" day. At the end of the day what ached most? It was my face from smiling. It was a fantastic day and one I will never forget.

Diane

Pink Baseball Caps

One day, my husband told me he was going to buy a Nuffield 10/60. I knew that it was a tractor but that was all I knew. This tractor was one of the first tractors he drove back in the mists of time. Then he decided that he needed the "full set" of five Nuffields. Naturally this was soon increased to about 35 tractors. He also subscribes to a couple of tractor magazines.

One day, he showed me an article in the magazine about the "Pink Ladies' Road Run". I said that I would like to participate in the road run, and told my daughter who also thought she would like to try it.

Some years ago, my husband's sister died from breast cancer at the age of 49, my sister contracted it at the age of 57. She is a survivor. We also have many friends who have had breast cancer, as well as many with other cancers.

We live on a caravan site in Essex, so we sent the husband out to buy a low loader so we could take a couple of his smaller tractors to Diss to take part in the road run. Naturally, the tractors were decorated in various shades of pink!

My daughter thought that the lady in front of us must know a lot of people as so many waves were being exchanged. Then she realised that the people watching the run were all waving to us! And as to when we went through Harleston! It brings tears to my eyes just thinking about it. So many people cheering and clapping. I felt like the Queen!

We were thrilled with the rosettes and medals we received after that first run, and added them to the tractors.

That year my brother gave each of us a pink baseball cap for Christmas, which became a great deal more important to us as he died the next year.

Every year after that we would get goose pimples as we saw the first tractors as we approached Diss, and indeed every time we talk about it.

The next year we brought three friends with tractors to the road run, fortunately one of them has a husband with a transporter so we could take all the tractors.

Then, of course, was the "Year of the Wet Knickers". It rained so hard that we all got soaked in the morning, but the sun came out at lunchtime so we dried off a bit in the afternoon. We said that if we had turned a corner and seen animals lining up two by two we wouldn't have been surprised!

We got into the habit that, the weekend after each road run, we would take the two tractors around the caravan site, with a lady carrying a pink bucket and she would explain what we had done and we raised a bit more money. We never had much difficulty in getting people to part with their money, due, I think to the fact that everybody seems to know somebody who has been touched by cancer.

Another year, one of our residents who has mental health problems joined us on the run. She also thought that it was an amazing experience.

As the years passed, we accumulated more rosettes and medals to put on the tractors.

Sadly, it came to the point when my husband could no longer strap the tractors on to the low loader so we had to retire from the road run, but we continue to donate.

Margaret

Thoughts from the Man at the Back

As the only male tractor driver that has completed every Pink Ladies' Tractor Road Run since the very first one, perhaps I should explain myself before the shouts of "Imposter, Drag Queen" or worse are directed at me. If I said that Annie had bestowed the title of "Chief Mechanic" upon me on that first run, I can establish a little credibility in my involvement in this tremendous event that has done so much good and raised so much money for breast cancer awareness and research.

And so, it came to be that on a dark and cold winters night in 2003, at Boundary Farm, a conversation took place between Annie and John around a roaring fire, fuelled by (I am told) just the one glass of wine each. Annie wanted a project and John had an idea. Some days later I was informed of a plan being formulated and immediately wanted to become involved. What could I offer to do to help with this fledgling idea that was evolving in the Chapman household?

Having spent a lifetime in agriculture I know a lot of tractor drivers. Most are male, a very few are female. I make this comment not as a sexist one but simply as a statement of fact. My thoughts were that a good many of the participants were not going to be drivers of tractors on a regular basis and even a brave few would never have driven a tractor before. What if they had problems during the run or their tractor broke down in full view of the onlookers? I offered to drive my tractor at the rear of the convoy and help anyone who required my assistance. Just by knowing that help was on hand, would I hope, give confidence and assurance to all those participating. My duties were extended to include lining the tractors up on arrival and giving a safety talk/what to expect on the day, some weeks before the event.

On that first run, 50 tractors raised £16,500. What a tremendous achievement, proving that the original concept had been spot on. A few breakdowns were encountered but nothing that could not be fixed and everyone made it round safely. There were many happy smiling faces and the mood was electric. What strikes me strongly is that the infrastructure put in place then has changed little over the years, suggesting that it was correct from the start, a tribute to Annie and John for their foresight.

Over the years I have been moved to tears many times by this event. The tremendous determination and courage of the participants and the support given by the general public as they clap and cheer and wave to us as we drive round the course. I see nervous ladies leaving Thorpe Abbot Airfield and see their confidence soar as they arrive at Gawdy Hall for the half way lunch break, their faces saying "Yes, we can do this"

On a personal level I have lost a mother and sister Eveline to breast cancer and sister Marg to kidney cancer. Having lost a mother and sister, Marg felt quite vulnerable and having attended a Road Run one year was overwhelmed with emotion and was determined to take part the following year. Despite being raised on a farm and doing her share of work there she was not a confident tractor driver but was determined to practice and become proficient at the task in hand. She did every run after that, till her illness and eventual passing prevented her from doing any more.

For me the Pink Ladies Road Run has had an enormous impact on my life.

Normally shy and reserved it has given me the confidence to carry out my duties in a way that would have been impossible for me earlier in life. I see the enormous effort that Annie and John put into this event every year. I see the difficult job that Chief Marshall Roger Connah does in organising all the marshals needed to stage this phenomenon and all those marshals doing sterling work at road junctions along the route. Me? Well, I'm last tractor round, by then the general public has been whipped up into a frenzy by the whole glorious event, I just ride around and bask in all the glory.

Robert

Research

I joined a trip to the Cancer Research establishment next to Addenbrookes at Cambridge a few years after the first tractor run and found myself in a minibus as the only chap with 15 ladies. I was unusually quiet in this company and enjoyed the journey with a group of mixed ages and backgrounds.

The introduction in Cancer Research was led by a professor who explained in detail with graphic diagrams how breast cancer arises and how it spreads. This was a moment of great emotion for me as I looked around and knew that several of my companions had had this awful disease and were in remission or even recovery. It must have been uncomfortable for them also to have to listen to a dispassionate discourse on the intimate development and progress of an infection.

The tour continued with an exploration of one of the laboratories where technicians and scientists were deep into the research. The equipment that was there involved costs of up to £250,000 for a single item and was far beyond our understanding. This research was revealing the origins of the cancer cells and enabling understanding of their growth.

I cannot say that I understood the process of the science but the quality of the work being done was clearly world leading. The updates of the equipment as knowledge is expanding will require more investment and the number of highly qualified people in the building need to be supported, and they made it clear to us that the funds raised by the Pink Ladies were valued both as an investment and in raising awareness.

I came home humble and with a greater understanding of why we are raising the cash at the Ladies' Tractor Road Run.

Roger

Some of the Support Crew: Michael Pointer, Keith Broomhall, John Chapman, Roger Connah, Rob White

Survivor

I don't have a huge story really.

I had breast cancer in 1999 and had a mastectomy but thankfully I am still here and OK so far!

I have supported breast cancer since and have just bought a pink poppy from Ipswich hospital in aid of the special breast care unit there.

Maybe I will join you this year

JANE G

The Road Run and My Roots

A decade and a half of asking friends, family and neighbours to sponsor me to do the Ladies' Tractor Road Run has brought an array of reactions. On the one hand there has been bemusement and fascination at something so unique and unusual, but on the other hand there have been more emotional responses, with so many affected by cancer in some way. For me, tractors and trips up to Norfolk have always been part and parcel of my life, but I too have had that personal connection to the cause, with the loss of my brother's partner, Jill, to breast cancer in 2009. The Road Run the following year, in 2010, was one that was particularly moving for me and my family.

But the Tractor Road Run is also an opportunity to connect to my roots. Over 35 years ago, I worked as a legal secretary in Norwich with a boss who was passionate about vintage tractors and combine harvesters – a boss called John Chapman. One of the joys then of taking part for me is to maintain this wonderful relationship I have with John and Annie which started all those years ago. Living down in Hampshire, it's their generosity in lending me one of their own tractors each year that has allowed me to get involved with something so amazing ever since I set my heart on getting involved when I came to watch way back in 2006.

With much of my family still based in Norfolk, it is also a lovely excuse to get us all together over a picnic at Gawdy Hall, the halfway point of the Road Run. No matter the weather, we make it work, even if it does mean my sister has to dash out on the Sunday morning to buy a gazebo to shelter us from the rain.

When I'm driving off-road with a long line of Pink Ladies and their tractors behind me, I find myself thinking about my father's cousin Auntie Doris, whose parents started farming at nearby Finningham in the 1920s and who ran the farm with them until 1961. As she lived until the age of 92, I was able to share with her the photographs of the first few Runs I took part in, and impress her with the fact that I too could handle a tractor. But I also find myself looking forward. When I did my first Tractor Road Run in 2007, my two sons were still at school. But now a Granny, I see my granddaughter Lily and also my nieces Ella and Millie as Pink Ladies in training, as I hope to pass on the great privilege of being a part of such a great community that contributes to something far greater than ourselves.

Alison

Mum

My Mum was the most incredible woman. She died of cancer in April 2019, 22 years after being given just two years to live as a result of a very rare blood disorder. During those 22 years, she lived life to the full – and was fortunate enough to be offered various trials, with some success – and carried on nursing, educating, enjoying life and her family. In fact, she was nursing and caring for others until she was no longer physically capable.

It was my darling Mum who first told me about the tractor run. It sounded like so much fun, but not having a tractor – or a brilliant driving track record! – I never felt I could take part. My son B, who is now nine years old, loved tractors (and still does now) and would play on my uncle's vintage tractors - sorry, Uncle Phil. My Mum always wanted to buy B his own tractor and shortly before she died, she sold her vintage MG car, to the ambulance driver on the way to hospital, so that she could make this dream a reality.

Not long after she died, a very rare 2-seater David Brown Cropmaster tractor was for sale locally. It was a beautiful rare tractor, with character, like Mum. My dad, another tractor enthusiast, bought it, and then last year I was able to do my first tractor run in memory of

my Mum. She always told me I could do anything and the whole day I felt her with me, cheering me on when I stalled in the ford; the rain was her tears of joy and the sun her warmth. She was there. I can't wait to do it again this year, in memory of Mum.

Lizzie

My Pink Ladies

Tractor Run Experience

I don't think I will ever forget my first tractor run.

My husband already owned a vintage tractor and I'd seen the run before but never thought of taking part (not sure why).

In 2015 I got talking to a fellow Pink Lady and she suggested I do the run, she said her husband would take me out on the road for some practice, so I signed up. Her dutiful husband duly took me out for about four runs on the road for some much needed practice.

The morning of the run came; myself and five other ladies left from Aslacton to travel along the A140 in a convoy to Thorpe Abbotts airfield for the start of the run.

We had been at the airfield for about one and a half hours when the rain started. And it continued and continued. I was soaked through to the skin (I was wet in places I didn't know existed), and I thought to myself, "My God, this is really miserable!" It was beating on my face, but when I got to Harleston I didn't care about the rain and the cold and being soaked, because the crowds and the people who had turned out in that awful weather started cheering and clapping for all of us. They made me forget about it all.

Once we'd got to Gawdy Hall it stopped raining and the sun came out. I had my husband bring me a change of clothes.

It was an experience of a lifetime, I haven't missed a run since, it's one of my favourite days of the year now, I love it. Every year when I do the run now I get really emotional and I'm usually crying going through Harleston, but I wouldn't miss it for the world. It's a wonderful experience for a very worthy charity.

I've also had the pleasure of being invited to Carfest, which we attended for three wonderful years, that's also a great privilege.

I can't describe in words what makes the run so special, is it the people, the sponsors, the joy and euphoria you get when people are cheering and clapping just for you? Well, I think it's a lot of all of that, and the pleasure you get from knowing you are helping to make the world a better place for women suffering from a terrible disease.

Sharon

Pink Ladies' Tractor Run 2021

What a wonderful display the Pink Ladies put on for everyone this year and a true tour de force of the resilience, resourcefulness and power of women. The weather was beautiful and many of us enjoyed picnics in the lovely Gawdy Hall meadow where the run stopped for a lunch break, giving us a chance for a closer look. After the long lockdown it was good to be out with so many people in the sun and exciting to see tractors of all ages and sizes arriving down the road towards us. The tractors seemed to stretch along the road for ages and just kept coming, far more tractors taking part than I had expected. So much work and imagination had gone into the tractor decorations which were stunning and made us all smile and I was told that some of the women had not even driven a tractor before. Among the smiles there were tears too, seeing tributes to people who are sadly no longer with us but are not forgotten. It must have been a long day for the Pink Ladies, with an early start and a long journey for some. Truly a memorable day and much appreciated by the spectators.

Juliet

Memories of the Pink Ladies

The first hint of something special was when we first moved into the area and one Sunday morning a number of tractors drove past the house decked out in ribbons and driven by ladies wearing the most ridiculous pink cowboy hats! After settling into village life we were introduced to the concept of the Pink Ladies the following summer and what an introduction it was! Standing in the grounds of Gawdy Hall I was truly amazed at the sight of the continuous stream of tractors coming into view, all driven by ladies and all magnificently decorated in glorious pink. As they came into the field I found tears rolling down my face whilst reading messages for loved ones lost to this terrible disease and pride for those who have survived.

In a strange way, the day is such an uplifting experience despite the sadness felt for those who are no longer here. It's a celebration of women and what they can achieve, it's a day for family and friends to be together and enjoy the wonderful spectacle of the Pink Ladies. As my husband said, "You girls certainly know how to do it!"

Lynn

Life!

My sister lives in Brockdish and I have supported the tractor run for a few years now and I have also had breast cancer!

On the day of my diagnosis, there was shock, not from me but from my consultant and support nurse, when without hesitation I said, "OK, please book me in for surgery."

"What, no discussion with anyone, do you not want to go and think about it?" Why? The diagnosis for a mastectomy was saving my life.

The day arrived and I presented at 7am on the day ward and was back home by 4pm with a glued-up operation site (no stitches), plasters, a list of exercises, a softie for my bra and a pink-striped heart cushion, the symbol of hope.

OK, so one boob less, how did I react? I took a good look in the mirror and accepted the new look as a hiccup on the path of life. I was still the same person apart from using a prosthesis, which incidentally I have cracked from ditching the NHS one and using one with very tiny granules, very comfy and cooling in summer.

I know there are many ladies who will be quite terrified by a breast cancer diagnosis which will change their appearance but the most important outcome is LIFE. Grab it with both hands and try not to regret the loss.

Janet

One Sunday in July

I was introduced to the Pink Ladies' Tractor Road Run by my sister-in-law, who in previous years I had sponsored and supported. But in 2016 an additional tractor was available, so this was the year I took part for the first time (and, unbeknown to most, I was in the early stages of pregnancy with my eldest!) And so now the road run is on my calendar every year.

The tractor I drive is a 1956 Fordson Major; it was the tractor that was in regular use on my husband's family farm back in the day. This, as well as another Fordson Major (which is what my sister-in-law drives) was restored by my brother-in-law.

I had two main goals when I started the tractor run. One: raise money and awareness for a fundamentally important cause. Two: I always hold the names of people I know who have been affected by cancer in my heart throughout the day. These two goals now are still very much the same, but to me it's so much more than these. It's part of being something so much bigger than I thought it would be.

For example, the day before the tractor run, me, my sister-in-law, our husbands, our children and friends gather together at our family farm in the afternoon and dress the tractors in pink together, before we put the kids to bed and have a well-earned takeaway and drinks. The day itself, before the tractor run sets off from the airfield, we greet familiar faces, we look for inspiration from other tractors for what we could do with ours the following year, and then we sit on our tractors, nervous and excited, as we wave farewell to our families until lunchtime as we set off.

I think for me personally (and I think this may be true for many other Pink Ladies), you cannot quite describe the sheer emotion you feel when you see how many people have come out into the streets, country back roads, fields, drives and gardens, to wait there and wave us all by. It's almost overwhelming, in the nicest way possible. Not only is this a true commitment on their behalf (there are easily over 100 of us Pink Ladies on tractors each year!) but we see them, year after year, supporting us, come rain or shine. To you all – thank you!

It's a joy to be able to take part in this incredible event. It feels like, for that one Sunday in July, everyone who is involved, everyone who takes the time to come and see us, everyone who donates, that we are all part of the same community with the same result in mind: to raise awareness about Breast Cancer. And I think, now more than ever, a little community spirit is a lovely thing to have, and it's something I am proud to be part of.

Rosie

Spreading the Word

It all started when I was a young 30-something embarking on a new life when my husband secured a job in the Middle East. We had to have medicals which were pretty thorough and part of the medical for me was a mammogram, never before had I had my boobs squashed and flattened in a vice. "Don't move" … move? I could just about breathe. However, the lady doing this squelching and pommelling of the said appendages was kind and understanding, together with being a font of advice for the future of these two (now very painful) breasts.

"Now my dear, you must check your breasts every month, do it on the first day of the month and you won't forget." As you can imagine, the question that spouted forth from me was "Why?" She explained that it would familiarise me with the feel of my breast tissue and I would quickly identify what is the norm for me.

Wise words that I have lived by for over 40 years, whether I was working and living in another country, volunteering or on holiday, I did the deed.

I remember being on a trek in the Himalaya mountains, waking up one morning in a tent with ice on the inside, fully clothed in yesterday's clothes, asking my tent mate what the date was … yes, it was the first of the month and my hands were frozen albeit tucked nicely in thick woollen gloves. A deep breath, and off came the gloves and the examination began, much to the consternation of the lady sharing my tent: "Heather, what on earth are you doing?"

After she got over the shock, she decided that she should do the same … only she did find a lump and we were still five days away from the end of the trek. We talked it through, she cried and howled like I had never heard before. I didn't know what to do to console her. Everyone in the camp heard the commotion and some of the other women joined us, with three of the five also having had breast cancer. It was a heart-stopping moment for me and I felt guilty advising her to check her breasts when she and I were having a ball of fun climbing steep slopes, crossing rivers, stumbling on remote villages and meeting some of the loveliest people you could wish to meet.

Somehow she and the rest of us got through that trek. We both gained a lot of friends and she gained a lot of support to carry her through a very difficult time in her life. She was in the middle of a divorce and was facing financial hardship. Never before had I experienced the kindness and support shown by those women who on that mountainside made it all ok and stayed for the long haul.

I felt a bit out of it, don't ask me why, but I felt a fraud being with a group of women who had all experienced breast cancer either personally or through a member of their family. They had all suffered one way or another. No-one I knew before that time had had breast cancer. I look back at me checking my breasts with regularity for years not expecting to find a lump, but doing it just in case.

A few years later I was volunteering in Kenya where I slept in a shed (boy have I slept in some strange places!) A group of four Kenyan women and two of us from the UK were sitting on the mattresses that were on the floor, we were discussing women's health and childbirth. A lump in the breasts was put forward as a topic. That evening it was discovered that two of the Kenyan ladies had previously found a lump in their breasts but didn't get it checked out because at that time they couldn't get free health care and they didn't have health insurance. With our help they were seen at a local hospital, one had a cyst and the other had breast cancer; she had her breast removed within a week. She wasn't given the option of a lumpectomy.

My own cancer story started in 2021. I had checked my breasts on 1 November, and thought "was that a small lump or am I being silly?" I let it go until 1 December. My GP was calm, but said, "We need to refer you to a consultant straight away. If you don't hear by 13 December, please let me know." I hadn't heard, the GP surgery chased it up and the first available appointment was 10 January 2022. I made the immediate decision to pay for a private consultation at the Spire in Norwich.

I had told no-one in my family, I only told three very close friends. I needed to deal with this and I wasn't going to be able to deal with the emotions of my family. I had to know where this was going and I wanted to be able to share a plan for the future, not get bogged down with emotion.

I had an appointment on 15 December. I was immediately sent for a mammogram, an ultrasound scan and a biopsy.

As soon as I saw the white blob on the screen I said to the doctor doing the scan, "That's cancer, isn't it?" She then scanned under my arm without confirming my observation. Then she said, "Let's do a biopsy." Back in with the consultant, and he confirmed that it was cancer, and that the results of the biopsy would be back on 22 December – three days before Christmas Day and it was the night I had invited all my neighbours to come to my garden and sing carols along with the Salvation Army band. Head held high, no tears (actually I haven't shed a tear), lots of love, and happiness at the thought of a Christmas with friends and family, the first in two years. Life had to go on.

The consultant had started to tell me the route things were going to take – MRI scan to see if there were any more cancers lurking in the breast, a lumpectomy, radiotherapy, and then Letrozole for the next five years. "Stop! Just take my breast off please, I don't go to topless bars any more and at 73 I don't need it for feeding babies." I had read a lot in the week from 15 to 22 December, to know that taking out a lump may not be the end of surgery on that breast. My mastectomy was planned for 12 January 2022.

Although the operation itself went very well, a few days later a haematoma formed. Fortunately a friend was staying with me and she called an ambulance which took me to A&E; six days later I was back in hospital for emergency surgery as the haematoma was till there and getting worse. The following day, I was home and I haven't looked back.

Family were shocked and upset that I had gone through this alone, but they all agreed it was typical of me and the right thing because they were emotional even though it was all over.

During these last few months, I have been using and following people on the Breast Cancer Care Forum, this has been invaluable in terms of advice and support.

Earlier this year a friend who has done the Pink Ladies' Tractor Road Run suggested that I join this wonderful group of ladies and raise some money for research into this awful disease, so here I am. Everything arriving at this house is pink, the charity shops in Diss are, I'm sure, fed up of me asking for pink things.

Together we can do this, we are survivors.

Heather

My Cancer Journey

It was November 2009. I had been studying for my Master's Degree in Health and Safety with Loughborough University, supported by my employer at the time. I was working as the Lead Health and Safety Advisor at the Norfolk and Norwich NHS Foundation Trust.

I had decided to take some time out after my work and study on a Saturday and go to Ickworth House to make a Christmas wreath from vegetation from the grounds with a lovely group of people. I came home to Brome with my wreath, of which I was very proud. Very grubby from handling moss, holly and a few snails I leapt straight in the shower … my life changed right there …

I have always kept a check on my breasts as per guidance and at 48 years old was too young for being part of the NHS mammogram programme. Soap on my hands, running them down my breasts and there it was. A small but definite lump. I was in shock and my brain went into overdrive. I kept feeling the lump but it was definitely not going away.

I finished washing, dried myself and can remember going downstairs and my late husband, Pete, knew immediately something was wrong. He was always someone who had the philosophy that worrying was not going to help and calmly said I would need to make an appointment for the GP when I told him and showed him what I had found. Not much sleep that night.

Next day I booked the appointment and got to see the doctor straight away. He found that the lump was moving slightly and tried to reassure me and say that it could be a cyst as it was moving. He advised waiting until my menstrual cycle was over again as it can be linked to the hormones.

A couple of weeks later and I was back, the lump was still there and I was referred to the Norfolk and Norwich University Hospital One Stop breast clinic the following week.

Simon Pain, my consultant, did the first check, I had a mammogram and because these were not conclusive, I had a biopsy of the lump. Anxious time then waiting.

The next day I was at my desk in the H&S office at the NNUH, my phone rang, it was Simon, who said: "Can you come across and have a chat about your results, Lynne?" That was the moment I knew that my cancer journey had begun.

Everyone was so kind and thoughtful but my husband was at home and I couldn't ring him to tell him the diagnosis as I was sobbing at this point. Simon made the call. A close work colleague called Maxine came to be with me and we had to go back to the office and tell my colleagues. It was all a bit of a blur from there and to be honest I can't remember the journey home except knowing that Pete was waiting for me at the door and we just hugged and cried together.

Not much sleep again but we talked and that helped. We knew that it would not be long before the operation to remove the lump but there were a few more scans, blood tests, lots of needles and poking and prodding before then.

I also had to go to my graduation ceremony at Loughborough University and was proud to receive my MSc in front of my husband and my Dad, however my "enemy within" as I had called my lump, was the unwelcome guest at the graduation.

I had stopped the tears very quickly and requested that everybody treated me as normal. I didn't want sympathy. My work colleagues were excellent and the in-house banter and jokes resumed. I quickly decided that Google searches about my cancer were banned and just used the expertise of the raft of specialists that were supporting me on my journey. The Breast Care Nurse team were really supportive and always responded if I had a question.

Each visit to the various departments for tests became a "moment". My MRI scan was my "Madonna Moment" as I dropped my breasts into what looked like top hats (rather than cones!)

My full body scan was my "beach moment" as I imagined seagulls and the waves rather than clanking machinery.

I had my "hot moment" when radioactive fluid was injected for another scan.

Positivity was my way of coping, anyone that said something negative or said, "Well, my friend had what you have and she did/said/felt …" was politely asked to go away.

Everyone has a different cancer journey and whilst support from others who had been through a similar journey was good, I was not going to do something on the basis that somebody else did.

Christmas came and into 2010 and my date was set to remove the enemy within.

My husband was very helpful in keeping my spirits up and insisted on waving a Mars Bar under my nose while I had been fasting since midnight and only on water!

I walked to the operating theatre, was given my gown, my paper knickers and my surgical stockings. That was such an attractive look, and being 5'2" and Simon, the consultant, being 6'7", was in stitches as I was standing next to him, laughing and saying I would never going to forgive him for the humiliation!

After the counting backwards for the anaesthetic to work, the next thing I remember was coming round and finding no drains fitted so I knew the cancer hadn't spread to my lymph nodes. Thankfully there was the option to remove the sentinel node at Norwich while I was under the anaesthetic and if clear then they did not have to remove the others.

When Simon came to see me on the ward he told me that my doctor was right, there was a cyst, but it was above the malignant tumour. However, the tumour itself was small and he had taken it all away. My enemy within had become my enemy without! However, bearing in mind it was January and very cold, I think the pain from my nipple being taped down was worse at the time than the scar.

That night I was listening to my Josh Groban *You Are Loved (don't give up)* and *You Raise Me Up* through my headphones and planning my escape from the hospital, I was determined that I wasn't going to be a patient lying around in my bedclothes. I had bought a front-buttoning cardigan that would allow the nurse access to see the wound, I was putting mascara on at 7am and had the requisite toast and tea and was not sick, and had the necessary pee before discharge could commence.

All was good regarding the wound, I had take-out medication and could go home to recover in my own bed.

From here on I kept up the attitude that I was now a cancer survivor not a cancer sufferer and was lucky as working in the hospital meant my appointments could be fitted around my working day.

I was then in the position of deciding if I wanted chemotherapy. I was not in the group where it would be definitely recommended and was not in the group where it would be deemed unnecessary. I saw this as another positive, I was back in control, not the cancer.

I weighed up the pros and cons, wrote it all down and decided that I would not have it. I was definitely having radiotherapy and my 17-session treatment plan was built up. Next step was the three tattoo dots to line me up. Also, the joy of knowing I had to stay the same size for the duration, diet on hold now after a bit of comfort eating!

I had the early morning slot, for which I will be forever grateful, as you can't use perfumes, soaps or deodorant when having radiotherapy. Lifting my arm to adopt the position for the "zap" was not as bad in the morning for the radiotherapist as it would have been after a day at work!

I had my treatment and then to enable me to make the transition from patient to staff member before heading back to the office, I went to the Big C Centre in the grounds of the hospital. Ironically, I had been part of the design when the centre was built due to my job, and here I was using it as a patient. This was particularly helpful and the staff there made my journey through treatment so much better.

Thankfully, I am now 13 years cancer free. I have regular checks and of course I continue my self-checking in the shower. Without that in the beginning my story may not have been so positive.

A big part of my support on the continuing journey, because the fear never goes away when you feel something out of the ordinary, has been being able to do the Pink Ladies' Tractor Road Run. So Many women coming together to drive a pink tractor and support the cause of breast cancer research.

I am lucky to know someone who unconditionally lends me his tractor each year to enable me to join the run, it is his way of supporting the charity and for that I am so grateful.

I love the buzz as we decorate our tractors as pink as can be and then set off on that 20-mile run, there are tears every year as these crowds line the streets and clap, wave and encourage us on the journey. Sun, wind or rain doesn't matter, we do it. I am so proud to be a Pink Lady, so proud to have been on radio and TV to promote the cause and tell my story. If it helps just one person to reach out, or check and find a lump that they can get sorted early, then it is all worth it.

Whilst this story describes my personal cancer journey, cancer has affected my life so much. I lost my Mum to secondary liver cancer when I was 40 and she was 68. My husband Pete had bladder cancer and sadly died just 12 months after his diagnosis in October 2013. My Dad died just nine months later from lymphoma, a blood cancer. I have also lost many other aunts and uncles from cancer. I have had many friends too that have been diagnosed, thankfully many have had treatment and survived like myself. Anything that can be done to research and help prevent cancer being so destructive has got to be a good thing.

Being positive I believe helps tremendously and I will continue to support and fundraise for cancer charities for as long as I am able to do so.

Lynne

Bah! to Cancer

My friend Kim is taking party in the tractor run and she asked me to send in my story.

I had a small tumour in my left breast detected in a routine mammogram nine years ago. After my surgery Kim was the first person to visit me. I remember it well as it was about four days after surgery and I thought I'd be fine, but was surprised how vulnerable and fragile I felt when we walked along Brighton seafront.

It was borderline whether I needed chemo, but I decided to go for it and then had radiotherapy. And then hormone therapy, which I'm still on. It was a hard few months but I read a great book which helped me get my head in the right place (*"How I said bah! To cancer"* by Stephanie Butland). I found the time when I was first diagnosed and waiting for the surgery the hardest psychologically.

Kim is a wonderful friend and I hope she enjoys the event as well as raising lots of money!

Janice

Penelope Pitstop

Brought up on a farm in Shropshire and marrying a farmer's son, perhaps it was inevitable tractors would play a part in my life, little did I know quite how much.

Whilst never directly involved in farming after my parents retired, I subsequently married a farmer's son, Keith. He wasn't interested in dairy farming and took the engineering route and lo and behold our first tractor – a Fordson Major E27N needing total restoration – arrived in 1979. Many additions to the collection followed courtesy of Cheffins Vintage Sales, including my International B414.

Back in 2000 Keith was encouraged to join a local group of like-minded men to form The Old Ram Tractor Club and I subsequently became the Treasurer. We became involved with a variety of events, including many road runs, and became interested in travelling a little further to participate in the annual National Vintage Tractor Road Run. This took place in a different county each year over the Easter weekend, and we often found ourselves taking our lorry with trailer and five tractors, with friends. We participated for nine years and The Old Ram Tractor Club hosted the event back in 2010 when 468 tractors participated!

Both Keith and I worked for agricultural companies through the years – Keith for Howards and then Dowdeswell before becoming self-employed – and myself for CLAAS for 35 years. There was always a connection with tractors one way or another.

I retired from CLAAS in 2015 and in the prior December and unbeknownst to me, my Pink Ladies' Tractor was brought down to CLAAS just outside Bury St Edmunds for the annual Pensioners Christmas Lunch which I usually organised and attended. Everyone in the company knew of Pink Ladies because of my annual request for sponsorship and the company decided to make the luncheon a special occasion for me. The men of the management team wore pink bow ties, the tables had a pink theme and the menu too, it was an amazing and emotional occasion.

In the first few days of each New Year, we have a tradition of taking our diaries and calendars and entering all known dates for events in the coming twelve months.

In this household this consists of many tractor events as we belong to quite a few clubs both local and national.

On 4 July 2004 there was to be a new and exciting entry – the first ever Pink Ladies Run.

How many would participate, where would we go, what would we wear, what if it rained, how would we dress our tractors? So many questions.

My 1962 International B414 is a great little tractor to drive and whilst red and pink might not be the ideal colour combination, it still looks very smart.

We owned a 16-seater trailer for a while, and I towed it on two occasions to enable friends to join the run but have to admit I had a very scary moment driving down Wingfield Road near the mill at Brockdish when the trailer was pushing me a little! On another occasion a steward missed directing me to turn left so I headed in the wrong direction! Thankfully the trailer would turn on a sixpence, so I was saved from total embarrassment.

Sensibly the use of trailers was soon stopped, there was enough to think about when already surrounded by relatively new tractor drivers.

Of the 17 runs I have missed just three – two due to family occasions, the third for a hip replacement which just couldn't wait any longer.

One of my favourite years was 2013 when I became Penelope Pitstop for the day. My husband Keith transformed my tractor into The Compact Pussycat, and I hired Penelope's costume. Speaking to friends at the start of the run, Keith was asked isn't Jane taking part this year? I was standing nearby; the disguise obviously worked.

Driving through Harleston is always the most emotional part of the day. The town is dressed carnival style and literally thousands line the streets clapping and cheering us through. I am always grateful for rain or sunshine – rain because no-one can see the tears, and sunshine because I can wear sunglasses.

Amazingly, statistics will confirm that we have been very lucky with the weather, though I do remember two

occasions when I was so grateful for friends bringing dry clothing to the lunch stop.

Statistics are also most relevant in respect of the reason behind our fund raising. I still remember the first presentation evening when a representative from Cancer Research spoke to us and advised that one in seven ladies would have breast cancer in their lives. I glanced around the room and realised that meant at least five or six of those present.

Having lost two dear friends to breast cancer there is an ongoing incentive to continue our fund raising. A feeling shared by so many ladies and hence the continuing appeal of our annual gathering.

Jane B

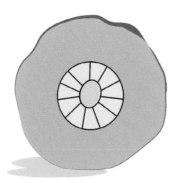
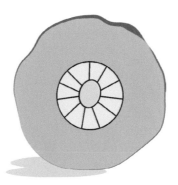
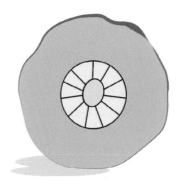

Pink Ladies' Toilets on Tour – The Toilet Man's Tale

The tale begins back in 2010. This was the year the Old Ram Tractor Club hosted the National Vintage Tractor Road Run. It took place over the Easter weekend with 468 tractors trundling around the Norfolk lanes.

The highlight of the run was the midday stop on Old Buckenham Common, a wonderful spectacle for the thousands of onlookers.

For this we needed to provide extra toilets at Tibenham Airfield, where we held the event; there would also be a need at the midday stop for toilet facilities.

Prior to this I was attending one of my favourite places, Cheffins sales ground at Ely. In the sale there were three toilets, idea … buy toilets, use for event, then sell again.

After some nodding and flashing of my bidding card I now had three toilets. Whilst admiring my purchases a young Irish chap walked up and opened a toilet door; I enquired what he was doing. Going to the toilet was the answer … thankfully he didn't.

A further three toilets were purchased by the Old Ram Tractor Club and after a little welding and metal bashing in my workshop, all six were mounted on a trailer which could be pulled by my tractor. The combination was used for the National Road Run at both the Airfield and the midday stop, just the job.

It was after the event that I received a call from Annie Chapman, of Pink Ladies fame; could she borrow the toilets for the Pink Ladies charity run and could I take them to Thorpe Abbotts Airfield for the start and then to Gawdy Hall for the mid-run picnic stop and subsequently back to Thorpe Abbotts?

How could I refuse? Can't sell the toilets now!

The toilets have now become a feature of the annual run. Painted pink with lots of balloons they make a great sight as I drive through the crowded Harleston main street with them towed behind my classic International B414 tractor. You could say it's the warm-up act before the main event – The Pink Ladies' Tractor Run.

On a different note, I am often asked about the practical aspects of this job, especially when the subject of emptying the toilets is broached (I have an electric pump!)

However, I am a farmer's son, and years ago our farm kept cows, pigs, chickens, and my sister's pony. Where there are animals there is POO, lots of it, so one becomes accustomed to forking, shovelling and spreading it. For the spreading operation our farm had a "vaci-tank" muck spreader, this would suck the liquid poo into its large tank which would then be driven to the field behind our tractor and spread on the fields. The poo became fertiliser.

As our farm was one of the first to have a vaci-tank, word soon spread of its wonderful suction properties. This was of special interest to all the surrounding houses with septic tanks.

To earn myself ten bob (50p today) back in the early sixties, I would arrive at the houses, the pipe from the vaci-tank was poked into septic tank, suction turned on and hey presto! septic tank emptied. Happy householder pays me the ten bob, whereupon I quickly drive tractor and vaci-tank away across the lawn leaving quite deep wheel tracks as the vaci-tank is now considerably heavier.

I would then spread the contents in a field farthest away from the farm and especially checking the wind direction whilst spreading!

Having just passed my driving test any chance to drive a tractor on the road, even for this job, was something not to be missed.

You will by now have realised that I am no stranger to the poo subject.

Finally, my engineering career culminated in the design and manufacture of my own range of agricultural muckspreaders, called the BIGMUK.

So, to summarise, it has been a life associated with poo and every July it carries on.

See you again in Harleston in July.

Keith Broomhall aka The Toilet Man

Secondary Sisters

I'm 34 and I love travelling, spending time with my friends and family, and my two beautiful dogs Tilly and Luna. I'm also living with incurable secondary breast cancer. This is my story.

At the end of 2013, I was travelling around Australia with my now hubby, Brad. It was the tri[p of a lifetime. But one morning when I was in the shower I came across a small pea-sized lump in my left breast. Breast cancer was the last thing on my mind. I thought only older women could get it. I'd never even been told to self-check and only found the lump by chance.

A few weeks later I went to see my GP. She wasn't concerned either, but referred me to the hospital just to be sure. And I'm so grateful she did. After an ultrasound, mammogram and biopsy, on 24 February 2014 I was told that the lump wasn't nothing. It was stage 3, grade 3 aggressive oestrogen and HER2 positive breast cancer. I was only 25.

The diagnosis absolutely floored me. How could this be happening? I was far too young and knew no-one else my age with breast cancer. I hadn't even told anyone other than my best friend about the lump, so it was a complete shock to my friends and family when I broke the news. I felt very alone and scared, as I now entered a new world I knew nothing about.

Over the next year it felt like I was on a rollercoaster consisting of chemotherapy, mastectomy surgery, hormonal treatment and regular injections. My friends and family rallied around to support me, coming to my appointments or just being there for me on the bad days. After I finished treatment, I was told I was in remission, so I began to rebuild my life and carried on working as a hairdresser. One new hobby was going to the gym to get my fitness back, and in one session I thought I'd pulled a muscle in my shoulder. But when the pain didn't go away for several months, I had to see if something else was wrong.

After a CT scan six months after the pain began, my oncologist told me that it was in fact secondary breast cancer in my bones. This is when breast cancer cells have spread to other parts of the body. In my case it had spread to my bones – over the whole of the ball joint in my shoulder, many parts of my spine and pelvis.

Secondary breast cancer is currently incurable. In that minute my whole world crumbled abound me. I was just 28, and I was facing a future with incurable cancer. I'd have to stop the job I loved so much, as a hairdresser. I'd never fulfil my dream of becoming a mum and the life I knew disappeared into thin air. Life was once again ruled by hospital visits and medical plans.

I had to have a major shoulder replacement followed by six rounds of chemotherapy. I was very poorly, and lost my hair again for the second time. I started having targeted therapy every three weeks in hospital, and remarkably after five years I am still on this to this day, and every three months I am scanned to check the cancer is still behaving. But – and this may surprise you – I feel lucky.

I never imagined I'd be here two years later, never mind five. I won't be cured, but I'm stable and my treatment is currently working. My life is very different from what I had planned or imagined but it hasn't been all bad. I have had amazing experiences that I'm so grateful for. Like having the most beautiful wedding and marrying my rock, Brad, in 2019, and I also wrote my Living List whilst in hospital recovering from my shoulder operation, a list of all the things I still want to do, to make the most of my life, and I feel grateful to have been able to tick off many of the activities over the last few years, from nice afternoon teas to abroad adventures and everything in between. Living and making memories with my loved ones is what keeps me here.

My diagnosis also led me to create my Instagram, @baldbooblesssandbeautiful. Cancer can be a lonely place, especially when you're so young. But by being open and sharing my story online, I met more people going through the same thing. It meant I felt less alone, and in turn I have helped others.

In 2019 I then met Nicky. We're the same age, both living with secondary breast cancer in our bones, and unable to have children. Our connection was instant. We could talk about things together that no-one else had truly got.

We wanted to create a place where other people like us could feel heard and understood, like we did when we found each other, so we launched the support group @Secondary.Sisters to show that although it's a hard place to be in, it can be wonderful as well.

The people I've met, the experiences I've had, and what I've learned about living life to the full, are things I can be thankful to breast cancer for.

With the havoc of the last few years, it's been amazing having experiences and things to look forward to. It helps to give me hope. And it's been incredible to meet the other models, and learn their stories. What's next for me? With my diagnosis, I try to be as upbeat and positive as possible. If I only have a short time here, I want to make the most of it. I'm busy making memories with all my loved ones. That's what gives me a reason to live.

My motto since I was diagnosed is: *don't worry about what you can't change*. Worrying won't make the cancer go away, so I try not to think about what might happen in the future. I'll deal with it as and when I need to.

Laura

I do like driving tractors!

Well, here I am sitting at my desk with pen and paper as Annie has asked all the pink tractor drivers if they could write a little something about why they do the tractor run. My reply to this question was, I'm really sorry, but it's pointless asking me as it would be a one-liner: "Because I like driving tractors …" But this got me thinking, while taking part this year in the 18th annual Pink Ladies' Tractor Road Run, I was sitting there driving the trusty steed that John had so kindly lent me, and my mind started to think about all the reasons as to why I take part.

Firstly, I must say that I take the fundraising very, very seriously. It is such a worthy cause and so many people have been affected by this condition, and I personally have several close friends that have been affected, and a couple that have lost their lives due to breast cancer.

I'm very fortunate that in owning a small business I am able to contact my customers personally and ask them for sponsorship. When I first took part in the road run I found it quite hard to approach people for money, but now I really find it quite easy as it is amazing how much people actually do want to give towards this cause, and their support is amazing. The ladies in my local village of Needham also hold a coffee morning to raise sponsorship for me, which is so kind and supportive of them.

Secondly, what a fantastic day it is to be able to get out on a tractor and see the overwhelming support of people throughout our journey around the villages. Although I have now done this run for seven consecutive years, the amount of support from people still manages to bring me to tears. As we go through the villages, thousands of people congregate in different places to watch the convoy. And then there are other people along the way, some

just standing on their own, some with neighbours and friends, all waving and wishing us luck. The support from people out there is absolutely phenomenal. I feel very proud to be a part of it all.

Hopefully one day I will own my own tractor, but until then I will continue to impose on John's kind generosity and loaning one of his for the day in order to continue fundraising with the rest of the pink ladies, the feeling of camaraderie amongst us all is fantastic and we all look out for one another during the day and have fun swapping ideas on how to decorate our trusty steeds.

So well done Annie, that certainly was a brainwave you had all those years ago, you are a fundraiser extraordinaire, and thank you to John for trusting me with his tractors, as: "I do like driving tractors"!

Helen

Get Checked!

I wanted to do the Pink Ladies' Tractor Run as I was diagnosed with ER positive breast cancer in 2016. I had a right breast mastectomy and immediate DIEP reconstruction. I then went on to take Tamoxifen for six years. I always like to help bring awareness and get women to check their breasts regularly, and to give back where I can, therefore I help run the Keeping Abreast Support Group. This is for ladies who have had or who are considering reconstruction because of breast cancer. They helped me when I needed it. I didn't check often enough until my friend of 40 years was diagnosed with triple negative breast cancer and just as she successfully completed all of her treatment, I got my diagnosis, but thankfully it was caught early, and that is key: if you have any concerns, get checked! Although unfortunately due to other health issues, after a practice on a tractor it caused me a great deal of pain, so sadly I had to back out of doing the run.

Tracey

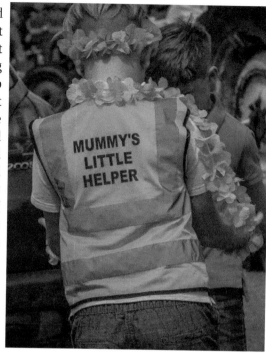

My First Mammogram

I had my first mammogram in 2001 at the mobile unit visiting Harleston, hoping (and expecting) everything would be normal. The results were not good – they needed some further testing as something had shown up. These further tests were carried out at the Norfolk and Norwich Hospital (the old one in St Stephens in Norwich) which showed I had a lump. This required biopsies to be carried out, which came back showing the lump to be cancerous so I would need a lumpectomy. My surgeon said it was deep so I would not have found it myself. Thank goodness I went for this, my first mammogram, as this most likely saved my life. As well as the operation, I also had a course of radiotherapy to make sure I was clear.

Since then, I have heard about the Pink Ladies' Tractor Run and thought, "This is something I would like to do to give something to Cancer Research UK for all the work they do to find a cure and/or treatment."

I've now completed several of these runs – the number of times escapes me – and enjoy the friendship and camaraderie of all the fellow ladies. These runs have not been without incident as I have broken down – but only twice!

As the total raised overall is approaching £1 million I hope to continue this in future years - me and my Little Grey Fergie.

Sue

2021 Maiden Voyage

I met Annie when I started working for Cancer Research UK in 2019. The Pink Ladies' Tractor Road Run was the event which I was most excited about because it sounded like lots of fun but also more importantly because of where the funds were restricted to.

In 2014, my Mum celebrated her 60th birthday. The next morning, she told my sister and I that she had breast Cancer. At first, the news was absolutely devastating. At the time I did not know that survival rates had doubled in the last 40 years. I just thought of the Big C and that cancer takes lots of people far too soon. My mum worked as a palliative care nurse at a local hospice for over 20 years, so we only heard about the lives that cancer stole. Fortunately for my family, they had found the cancer early at a routine mammogram (which my mum nearly didn't attend because she thought she would be OK). My mum had an operation which removed the tumour followed by a course of radiotherapy. We were lucky, but there are so many families that haven't been as fortunate as mine.

In 2021, I asked Annie if she had a spare tractor as I really wanted to take part in the run! I learnt to drive a tractor (a big thanks to John who is so patient!) and then I was ready to go. It was such an incredible day! Firstly, I was a little worried when we arrived at Thorpe Abbotts and it started to rain, I really did think I would get very soggy. However, then the sun came out which meant we could go through Harleston in the glorious sunshine and enjoy a fabulous picnic at Gawdy Hall. I honestly cannot describe the feeling of driving through Harleston. There were so many wonderful people who came out to watch us which was very emotional. It is definitely terrifying trying to drive a tractor in a straight line! Annie and the Pink Ladies are so committed to funding research and beating breast cancer, it was such an honour to join them, and I cannot wait to do it again

Debbie

Tractor Decorating Team – 2022

Every year our friend Jane drives a vintage Massey Ferguson in the Pink Ladies' Tractor run and this year she decided to trust the decoration of the tractor to her friends – little did she know!!

Over the years Jane has collected a range of pink ribbons and flowers which were passed over to us and we started to plan exactly how we would decorate the tractor. In particular we wanted to decorate the top of the bonnet, which had not been done before, and the creative member of the team, Lynn, came up with the idea of a blanket of woolly pompoms. So her long winter evenings were devoted to making hundreds of pompoms (all shades of pink of course) ably assisted by Sydney her cat. The pompom production was so successful they spread from the bonnet of the tractor to the front wheel hubs and to the toy box of Jane's two dogs.

Like any lady who is having a new outfit, a fitting was required for the tractor. Therefore, Richard, who generously lends the tractor each year, allowed us to visit his barn and take the tractor's vital statistics. Having carefully measured the size of the bonnet, counted the number of holes in the wheel hubs suitable for attaching decorations and determined how many yards of ribbon would be needed, we returned home to prepare for Decoration Day.

On Saturday morning we arrived at Jane's house with all the decorations to dress the tractor ready for the Pink Ladies' Run the next morning. The decorating team were climbing all over (and under) the tractor to attach flowers, ribbons, tinsel, rosettes and special poppy pictures drawn by the youngest member of the decorating team, Florence. As you might expect there was a great deal of laughter and the atmosphere of everyone joining in meant that even if you weren't driving the tractor, you were taking part.

Sunday morning, the weather was great (we could now uncross our fingers) and we set off for Gawdy Hall and the Pink Ladies' picnic – we arrived at 12.30pm with the Pink Ladies expected at around 1.00opm. The picnic is always popular but this year the turnout was exceptional. The meadow was full of families having a lovely time with the ice cream van doing a roaring trade – and of course not forgetting the essential pink portaloos.

As 1.00pm approached all eyes started watching the far side of the meadow looking for a glimpse of the first tractor – and here they come. The first in a procession of over 100 decorated tractors enters the meadow to take their place in an impressive line-up; each one is greeted by the crowd with waves and smiles, knowing that the Pink Ladies make a difference to Cancer Research each year.

This year we were able top spot Jane's tractor easily as it was the only one covered in pink woolly pompoms!

Lizzi

2010

I took part in my first Pink Ladies' Tractor Road Run in 2010. I knew nothing of it until Penny (another Pink Lady) asked if she could borrow my husband's 1966 MF135 for that year's run. She was subsequently given one for a special birthday and no longer required Martin's. By this stage I had found out what the Pink Ladies was all about and was keen to participate myself. The first hurdle to overcome was to learn how to drive it! Luckily I was in the hands of my would-be farmer husband who was happy to teach me. I was not a very confident pink lady on that first run and didn't really look the part, not realising how much everyone went to town decorating themselves and their tractors. Hopefully I've made up for it since and have now enjoyed participating in ten road runs, my most recent raising a personal record amount.

I tragically lost my best school friend, Jane, to cancer. She was only 40. Similarly, two other friends, Gill and Richard, who also died from the disease, both also 40. I remember these friends on my runs as well as others and family members who I have lost through cancer. I feel privileged to be a member of the Pink Ladies and able to fundraise for such a great cause. Thank you to Annie and her team for organising such a worthwhile, and at the same time, enjoyable event.

Ginny

Tractor Drawing by Florence age 10

Press Release, Eastern Daily Press, 2021

Pink Ladies' Tractor Run is back!

The iconic Pink Ladies' Tractor Road Run is set to return in style as the group looks set to hit a fundraising total of more than £¾ million.

With last year's main event cancelled due to the pandemic, this year's run will take place on Sunday 4th July with a convoy of around 112 tractors.

Since it began in 2004 the events has raised more than £734,000 in aid of Cancer Research UK's breast cancer appeal and this year the Pink Ladies hope to smash through the £¾ million mark.

Organised by Annie Chapman BEM, the annual run will wind its way through south Norfolk and north Suffolk on a route which starts at Thorpe Abbotts airfield. It then heads through Thorpe Abbotts, Brockdish, Upper Weybread and Harleston for about 12.30pm, before stopping for lunch between 1pm and 3pm at Gawdy Hall Meadow, Redenhall.

The route back to Thorpe Abbotts airfield heads to Pulham St Mary, and then through Rushall, Langmere Green and back to the airfield for about 4.30pm.

Annie Chapman said: " It's wonderful that this year's event is going ahead, I'm so pleased for the ladies who were so disappointed last year. Cancer Research UK has suffered so badly with events being cancelled and the efforts these ladies make for the charity are brilliant.

"I've got some very excited ladies I can tell you that – it makes all the hard work worthwhile.

"We believe in these ladies, and we would really like to get to three-quarters of a million this year. We've raised more than £734,000 so far and because it's been given over a period of time it's been a gradual build up – there's an element of excitement because of the amount of money raised for this cause.

"Everybody knows somebody affected by this cancer, it's at the forefront of everyone's mind. It's very scary and sadly we have lost a lot of ladies over the years to breast cancer and that's why we keep going.

"The event is the most humbling experience, it rea⬛ has been the best thing I've done in my life."

Jane Broomhall, who lives near Long Stratton in so⬛ Norfolk, has taken part in 14 of the runs. She sa⬛ "When the first Pink Ladies' Tractor Run was held⬛ 2004, it was a unique opportunity to raise money ⬛ breast cancer research and, we thought, a one-off eve⬛ we all knew of someone who was receiving treatme⬛

"Over the years the Run has become an annual trib⬛ by participants to both those we love who have surviv⬛ but also to those ladies we have loved and lost – ⬛ me, my closest friend in 2015 and, just two weeks a⬛ another close friend. We can never do enough."

This year more than 30 ladies new to the run will ⬛ taking part, including the Beat Manager for So⬛ Norfolk rural crime, PC Sue Matthews – on a pol⬛ tractor.

Debbie Adams, a Relationship Manager at Can⬛ Research UK, is also taking part for the first time. S⬛ said: "I am so excited to be taking part in the Pi⬛ Ladies' Tractor Road Run for the first time. The Pi⬛ Ladies are an inspiration and I am so thrilled to ⬛ joining them and helping hit the three-quarter milli⬛ milestone!

"Breast Cancer research is a cause close to my hea⬛ My mum survived a breast cancer diagnosis six ye⬛ ago due to early diagnosis and to research. I want ⬛ raise as much money as possible for Cancer Resear⬛ UK, so more women survive their diagnosis."

In 2020 a smaller tractor run took place in Septemb⬛ once the lifting of restrictions allowed for groups ⬛ up to 30 to meet. Annie said: "We had to cancel la⬛ year's event but in September we held a mini-run wi⬛ 30 ladies socially distanced, people were brilliant a⬛ stood in groups watching, everyone was careful.

"Because we couldn't do the run, I put a challenge ⬛ to the ladies to fundraise in different ways. A fam⬛ from St Cross South Elmham organised their ow⬛ tractor run for their family bubble and held a great b⬛ sale on a local meadow, another lady did a sponsor⬛ ride around her garden on a child's pedal tractor, o⬛

group did a mini-run near Mendlesham and another group displayed their tractors in Aslacton.

"It was just brilliant, everyone was using their initiative, all in all we raised more than £28,000 and we didn't expect to get anything after the main event was cancelled.

"As with any event of this size it cannot be achieved without the support of many people. I would like to express my thanks to all tractor owners, landowners, the many marshals, collecting ladies and anyone else who helps to make this event happen, it's a large team effort!"

Kate

The 2012 Ladies' Tractor Road Run

As a relatively new resident of Suffolk, and a total newcomer to country life, I was nevertheless persuaded, in a weak moment, to become a "Pink Lady" and take part in the 2021 Ladies' Tractor Road Run on Sunday 1 July 2012!

Diane Poppy, of Lime Tree Farm in Stoke Ash, had rashly agreed to lend me one of her tractors (she was also driving another tractor on the day, even older than mine and with no cab at all) and was brave enough to give me a driving lesson beforehand – not easy as I'd never even sat on a tractor before! So, after a short practice steering it around the outside of her barns and only having gone forwards, I had a very short practice on proper roads and finally managed to get it above second gear! The large notice on the inside of the door telling me what to do when (not "if") the tractor turned over didn't instil me with confidence … but nothing ventured, nothing gained.

1 July dawned with periods of sunshine interspersed with overcast periods and a fairly consistent wind (which played havoc with my long pink wig)! Greg Aldridge, also from Stoke Ash, had kindly transported our tractors in advance to a farm near the start at Thorpe Abbotts Airfield, and the morning's route took us via Brockdish to Harleston where we stopped for a picnic lunch at Gawdy Hall Meadow. After a short break, we set off again returning via Pulham St Mary, Rushall, Langmere Green, arriving eventually back at Thorpe Abbotts Airfield.

The atmosphere throughout was wonderful – every village we drove through had people sitting on garden chairs at their gates, waving and clapping and encouraging us, with pink balloons fixed to hedges, and banners and messages. In Harleston, the biggest town we drove through, we had to go up the main street (weaving through the parked cars with on-coming

traffic dodging into gaps) and the people were three deep on the pavements cheering us on and waving.

We were supported throughout by signs and arrows for us at all the corners and marshals at any junctions, either holding up the traffic or waving us through when it was safe. The whole day was very well organised – just as well with 136 mainly ancient tractors, many of which were obviously very treasured and loved. Lots of the tractors had no cabs and the lady drivers were totally open to the elements. Mine had a cab, but Diane had arranged for the doors to be taken off for the day, as she said, "So that you can enjoy the atmosphere of the crowds". I think she just wanted to ensure I got as wet and cold as the rest if it rained! Many of the younger girls were in T-shirts and must have been frozen but those of us who were more mature were better attired for the weather - I didn't take off my fleece all day! But it was pink and white stripes and I had a long pink wig on and pink fishnet fingerless gloves to finish the ensemble.

We (and all the other drivers) had spent several hours decorating the tractors with flowers, banners, balloons, ribbons, anything pink basically, and I was amazed how well the decorations stayed on despite there being not a lot of things to fix them to! And we had to be careful not to block air inlets or exhaust chimneys … and keep clear of the moving parts … so much to think about! But it stayed dry!! My ribbon flowers even stayed on the big back wheels despite our having to drive through a stream/ford on the first section of the route.

By the end, I felt much more in control of my machine. But I still reserved a couple of very dramatic kangaroo-style gear changes for those bits of the route where most people were watching! (If some of the spectators had realised how little practice a lot of us had had, I'm sure they wouldn't have been so relaxed by the roadsides!)

Annie Chapman, the lady who organised the whole event, had already raised £223,000 in the past eight years and the 136 ladies this year incredibly raised £48,000 with the help of their own individual sponsors, and therefore the total raised to date by the Ladies' Tractor Road Run now exceeds a quarter of a million pounds! In recognition of her huge contribution to Cancer Research UK through her previous Tractor Road Run fundraising, Annie was nominated by the charity and carried the Olympic torch through Aldeburgh in Suffolk on 5 July. She has said that she considered this a huge honour but that "I will be carrying the torch not for me but for all my pink ladies, past and present, for the tractor owners, the backup team and helpers, the landowners, the incredibly generous people who have sponsored our run and for those brave ladies who have had to come to terms with breast cancer. You are very special and inspirational people and you have made the Ladies' Tractor Road Run a very special event."

I feel privileged to have played a small part in this year's event and found the whole day to have been a fabulous experience! I recommend it to any other brave ladies who get an opportunity to take part.

Pam

Poppy

The first I heard about the Ladies' Tractor Road Run was from my friend Christine. I had become friendly with Christine and Ralph after discovering a family connection when looking at my family tree. Christine had taken part in the very first road run, and she was very enthusiastic about it. As I possessed a tractor I agreed, so in 2005 I ventured out along the back roads, not having driven a tractor very much for some years and not really knowing the way to the field where we were meeting. Luckily I reached the venue with no mishaps and in time to decorate the tractor.

In the following years we became more organised. I was joined by friends and family and Greg, who lived in the village, was a great help to us, often lending a tractor and providing transport, with a low loader trailer carrying two tractors and pulled by a third. My daughter drove twice and one year I shared a two-seater with a friend, which was good as we were able to share the driving and chat on the way round. One friend, who took part in 2010, subsequently did not survive breast cancer.

Perhaps the most memorable year for me was 2012. I was driving an MX 35X. This tractor was purchased new by my father, Fred, in 1963. She was for many years used on the farm for straw and corn carting, and rolling and harrowing the fields, before becoming too old and being left standing in the cart shed and almost abandoned.

Then in about 1990, my cousin Mike started a venture rearing ducks, in the middle of Thetford Forest, and he needed a tractor to run his electricity generator. My father gave him the MX 35X, and he named her Poppy. For many years Poppy did an invaluable job running the generator, until Mike retired in 2011. Mike wanted her to stay in the family so he gave her to another cousin, John, who farmed at Billingford. John gave Poppy a complete overhaul and repainted her. She looked splendid, and I was allowed to drive her on the Road Run in 2012, when we featured in the "Tractor" magazine in October that year. This was particularly poignant as John died the same year from cancer (not breast cancer). Poppy was subsequently bequeathed to John's grandsons, so she still remains in the family.

I think without exception we all enjoyed the Pink Lady experience, the fantastic reception we received driving through Harleston and the picnic lunches in the meadow at Gawdy Hall. And of course we helped support breast cancer research at the same time.

Diane

Dad's Idea

Cancer has touched my loved ones a number of times over the last few years, my friend passed in 2021 aged 51, from a short illness, my beloved aunt Rosie, who was like a sister to me passed away in 2018 aged 55, only ten weeks after diagnosis, both left children, who as young adults are wonderful, hardworking and kind, their mums would be proud. My husband has fought cancer and so has, more recently my dad.

It was my dad's idea to do the Pink Ladies' Tractor Run, a tractor owner and enthusiast. He wanted to remember his sister Rosie with something meaningful, joyful and fun. My friend Shelly and I have been friends since four years old and I couldn't think of anyone better to do the run with, what a wonderful experience to learn to drive a tractor! I was doing well until we agreed the tractor I had been practising on was going to be very slow, so only a few weeks before I changed from an Allis B to a Fordson Major … I must admit I felt a little wobbly about it! However, after a few sessions, lots of encouragement and advice, I felt much more relaxed, though not sure my dad did!

The run was honestly, one of the best experiences of my life, it meant lots of time with my friend, built my confidence, brought me so much fun and joy and most importantly raised lots of money for much needed research into cancer. The day was so well organised, I felt supported and safe and the drive through Harleston was very emotional and really reminded us all about why we did it … I can't wait for next year! Thank you for organising.

Sarah

Proud Pink Lady

My Pink Lady journey began in 2013; I had seen reports of the run the previous year and thought it a marvellous venture. Having my own vintage tractor and trailer, and not averse to a bit of a jolly, I considered the run to be an excellent event, particularly as it raises money for such a fantastic cause and one that is close to my heart, having had several friends (male and female) that have been affected by breast cancer.

I trooped up from Hertfordshire to join the run and could not have foreseen then how important it would become, and how warmly I would be welcomed by Annie and Libby into the "family" of the Pink Ladies.

When Annie was invited to take a team to Carfest by Radio 2 DJ Chris Evans, I eagerly put my name forward and have attended these since, ensuring that the Pink Ladies are represented at such a prestigious and fun event. The tractors are always greeted so warmly by all attendees, public and celebrities alike – they cannot fail to raise a smile dressed in their finest pinkness!

I am proud to be a Pink Lady tractor driver, am thankful for the friendliness shown by all participants and am humbled by the amount raised by my fellow drivers and the support given by the spectators and supporters who complete the event. Onwards to the million!

Tamsin

On Sunday, first one of July

On Sunday, first one of July, Pink Ladies mount their steed
Tractors of just every kind, no matter what their speed
Big ones, small ones, old and new, some that now quite rare
Pimped up pink, with bows and frills, no longer mud they wear.

Excitement mounts for half past hour, get ready for the start
Balloons attached, bunting tied, photos close to heart;
Tutus on and angel's wings, plus bras of every size,
Cancer Research banner raised, to rally as it flies.

Must not forget as women all, and most of certain age,
That handy little tag along – those "loos upon a stage" –
Last minute dash before they're called, to turn their engines on
No chance there'll be to stop enroute – observers all along.

Annie leads from up the front, with Libby close behind,
The muster shout then moves them off, in strictest order mind.
As "tractoring" through country lanes, folk bless all with their cheers
The clapping and encouragement still ringing in their ears.

At Harleston crowds grow very thick, with streets lined side to side,
It takes some mettle driving straight, as tears they fight to hide.
Emotions of the day rise up, with thoughts of those they've lost;
To help raise funds for this great cause, will never draw a cost.

Onwards go to Gawdy Hall where friends and family wait,
Broad smiles are seen on drivers' face as they head through the gate.
Picnics made and rugs laid out, time spent with those held dear;
A day of making memories, with purpose that is clear.

Back they go across the fields, with marshals waving through,
Roads are closed so run can pass, by all this kindly crew.
And all of those who lend support, to jump start, fix or tow,
Grateful thanks for all their help, can only ever grow.

And then return to Abbotts field, conquerors to base;
Weary – just a little bit, but grins still on their face.
To dismount now and find a place for final photographs,
Clamber up onto the bales, a sight for many laughs.

The photo took and thanks all round, stories from the day,
Now drive their charges back to home or load and haul away.
Thoughts will go to what's been raised, to each and every pound,
And what they'll add to decorate when next year comes around.

Tamsin

Tractor Run Memories

My first memory of the tractor run was watching it, with my family, go through Alburgh (pre 2011). Having known Annie and several of the Pink Ladies for many years, through Harleston Players, it was perhaps inevitable that I would be persuaded to give it a go. To be fair I did not need much persuasion. I still get as excited now as I did then to be a part of this incredible event. My hero has to be Roger who provides my tractor each year.

So my first run was 2011 and I have been fortunate enough to take part in all the subsequent runs, including the breakout in 2020 where, due to Covid, there were only 30 tractors allowed. My family have always been my biggest supporters and so it was extra special this year to have my daughter Elizabeth on the tractor behind me. She was just nine when I took part for the first time and she has always wanted to be a part of it. Thanks to John having a spare tractor this year her dream came true.

Over the years the weather has tended to be kind but who can forget 2015? It poured all morning and by the time we all arrived at Gawdy Hall even our underwear was soaked. Luckily most of us were met by family with a complete change of clothes (apart from Pat, whose husband Andy kindly donated his own trousers and returned home in his underpants), hot coffee and picnics which we ate in our car.

Another rain soaked memory for me was 2018 at Carfest South. I was so lucky to be able to join Annie and Julia that year – Julia and myself were to be flag bearers in the parade on the Sunday morning. It had started raining on the Saturday, and by Sunday it was rather damp!

Of course the reason we all do this every year is to raise money for cancer research. Cancer affects all of our lives in some way, either directly or indirectly. We all know someone who has been diagnosed with cancer, my father at the age of 85 has been diagnosed with three different types since 1995. Just recently two of our "sisterhood" (a bunch of theatrical luvvies) have been diagnosed with breast cancer. The fight goes on.

Raising money never stops, it is not just the sponsorship for the day itself. In 2012 I directed Calendar Girls for the Harleston Players and we did our own calendar to raise money. The profit from this was split between Leukaemia Research and our Pink Ladies fund, with many of the Pink Ladies featuring in the calendar and the play. Oh what memories!

Sara

For Gunvor & Rachel

My story for you is that Rachel is the daughter of my best friend Gunvor. Rachel had breast cancer in 2018 and went through operation and treatment and recovered well and was given the all clear. Sadly Gunvor passed away in November 2021 from pancreatic cancer after a short illness and a group of us with the family have been raising money for cancer research in memory of Gunvor and in support of Rachel. Rachel was going to do the Pink Ladies' Tractor Run in July 2022 but unfortunately her breast cancer returned and she could not take part and I was asked to take her place at the last minute. Luckily I have driven tractors since a young age and I was confident to take part. I loved every minute of it and was very proud to take part in memory of my dearest friend and in support of Rachel. I hope to take part again next year.

I am working on a friend, Geoff, to buy another tractor so Rachel and I can do the run again next year!

Jenny

The Road to Recovery

We are all tractors, born brand new
Shiny and pink
But
We get older
Things stop working
Parts need replacing
The oil keeps dripping
The wheels stop turning
And then the tractor breaks down
We've stopped.
Stuck.
There is no moving forward
Or back
Everything is
           Falling
                      Apart
But people are coming to help
To push
And pull
           Roll
And carry
              Forwards

The road to recovery is long
And there may be spanners in the works
But one day that same tractor
Will lead the way
Shining pink once again
And we will prove that
Nothing is impossible

And we will keep riding the road to recovery
Until everyone has crossed the finishing line.

Charlotte (Aged 14)

Toy Tractor Run

Sunday 5 July 2020 was the perfect tractor run day. The weather was hot and sunny but because of Covid-19, the world had been turned upside down and like many events in 2020 and 2021, the tractor run was cancelled. A couple of days prior to the projected date, Annie emailed her pink ladies with her inspirational speech encouraging ladies to fundraise where possible and continue to fly the flag! I read the email to my husband Mark and he jokingly said that I could do my own tractor run in the garden instead. The cogs turned while I churned it over and I said: "Actually, why not?" It seemed the perfect idea given the circumstances. I straight away took to social media and set up a fundraising page. By this time, it was the day before the intended date. The response was fantastic with donations coming in left right and centre, many of whom were from people I didn't know but who religiously supported a Pink Lady every year.

On Sunday 5 July, I did my own garden tractor run on my children's toy tractor. We decorated her in the normal pink fashion all ready for her maiden voyage. I even put my Pink Ladies outfit on for the ride!

I did my 100 laps of the patio, many of them towing a toy trailer with one of my children in it, which was actually much harder on the legs than the real tractor run! My husband did film extracts and Facebook Lives to promote the garden run far and wide bringing more sponsorship in lap by lap. After which, Mark decided he would have a go and see if we could raise some more! So off he went and wore his pink shirt and my pink wig (becoming an honorary Pink Lady) and did yet another 100 laps of the patio.

We were able to raise a good sum of money for Cancer Research UK on a bit of a whim.

Prior to the garden run, I had done the tractor run twice before and then again in 2021. Last year was a particularly poignant year for me in doing so. A good friend of mine was diagnosed at the age of 39, and that truly brought it home about the importance of what we are doing.

Meryl

My Beloved Nuffie

I first drove in the Pink Ladies' Tractor Road Run in 2007, a few years after it started. I heard some of my friends in Harleston Players talking about it and asked Annie if I could join that year. I borrowed a tractor from John Chapman, an International with a cab I think, but I could be wrong. So a few pink decorations and me in pink and off I went. It was really quite moving seeing all the people cheering us on.

The next year John asked if I would be able to drive his Nuffield, after a lesson or two I felt competent to drive her, she's a heavy beastie with a hand throttle. I strove to decorate her as much as I could, so she was covered in flowers. That year without the cab on I couldn't believe the difference, *hearing* the people along the route cheering and clapping and so appreciative of what we were doing. Every year since, bar two, I have driven my beloved Nuffie (OK, she's John's) and have been brought to tears by the people who sponsor us, who line the streets, have parties in their remote gardens in the countryside, who cheer us on.

This year was especially moving as two more of our friends have had the dreaded diagnosis but thanks to the research enabled by the money we get from our drives, these friends will have a good outcome. There was also the most brilliant handwritten sign on our journey. A young woman stood with her young family cheering us on next to a sign she had written on a big piece of cardboard, it read: "Thank you ladies, I am a survivor". My goodness, I could barely see to drive. That really brought home the importance of what we do, simply by driving our beautiful old tractors bedecked in pink we are helping to save lives. Makes you think, doesn't it?

Dawn

Pink Sheep

I became a pink lady for the first time back in 2014. I remember the previous year that I had been at Woolpit Steam Rally exhibiting my Massey Ferguson 35x, when I saw a lady with a Fordson Dexta which had a poster on it about the Pink Ladies' Tractor run. Once I had seen the poster I knew that I wanted to be a part of the event, so planned on getting booked in for the following year, which is what I did. I still wish that I had known about the tractor run sooner, as I most certainly would have been a part of it beforehand.

In 2014, I took part in the tractor run for the first time using my Massey Ferguson 35x. This tractor will always be very important to me not just because it was the first vintage tractor that I owned but because it is now run in memory of my late grandfather Tommy Tween, who purchased the tractor for me originally. I remember feeling quite nervous about the event and not really knowing what to expect or whether I had "pinked up" my tractor enough, although I don't know what I was worrying for really, as I soon made friends with the ladies driving the tractor near me, which calmed my nerves.

The 2015 tractor run for me can only be described as the "soggy knickers" year. It was the wettest tractor run that I have ever taken part in! I believe that I changed clothes at least twice and at Gawdy Hall I was very thankful that my dad hadn't got round to clearing out his truck of everything, as I done the second half of the run wearing one of his boilersuits and his waxy jacket (still with wet knickers!)

Later in 2015 when I visited a farmer in North Lopham, Norfolk, I fell in love with a Massey Ferguson 135 with a Lambourne cab, that was sat in the corner of his shed. We had only visited the farm to purchase a straw chopper, but I couldn't help but to take a closer look at the 135 in the shed. Ken was quite clear that the 135 was not for sale and would always stay on the farm as it had been there since it was roughly six months old. I chatted to Ken for quite a while about vintage tractors and explained to him that I had taken part in the Pink Ladies' tractor run for the last two years. When we left the farm that day after purchasing the straw chopper, Ken said that I needed to go away and think about making him an offer for the 135. I couldn't believe that it was thanks to Pink Ladies that he was considering

selling the tractor to me. I made him an offer which he agreed and in October 2015, I was the proud owner of said 135. After a speedy restoration in 2016 I was able to do the tractor run with my 135. I invited Ken to come and see her at Pink Ladies and it was so lovely to see how proud he was that his tractor was taking part for such a great cause.

I feel very privileged to own my own vintage tractors and Pink Ladies will always firmly be in my calendar every year. My 135 usually stays "pinked up" all year round, so that I am able to fundraise at whatever tractor show I take her to, although 2022 meant that I also did extra fundraising with the pink sheep at Kent County Show, which you may have seen at Gawdy Hall for the picnic.

I was talking to my friend Tory at the Norfolk Show and got onto the subject of pink sheep. I loved the idea and straight away ordered six cans of pink hairspray and hoped that they would arrive by Saturday so that the pink sheep could happen. The pink hairspray arrived

and Ben chose the sheep in question. We used all six cans of pink hairspray much to the disgust of the newly neon pink sheep! On the day, due to the heat, the pink sheep was not keen on being out in the middle of the field, so spent most of her time hiding in the shade with her non-pink friends. However, many people did get to spot the pink sheep on the day of the tractor run, and some of the residents' children of Gawdy Hall after the tractor run went out every morning to spot the pink sheep.

The following weekend we were going down to Kent for the Kent County Show, to show some of Ben's Jacob sheep. Ben contacted the chief sheep steward and asked if the pink sheep could come along with us to do a some extra fundraising, and she said yes. The pink sheep had faded slightly during that week due to how hot it had been; therefore, I had ordered another two cans of pink hairspray just to do a touch-up paint job to make her neon pink again. However, things didn't quite go to plan on the Friday morning before we headed off to the Kent show. Ben caught the pink sheep and tied her up on her trimming stand so that we could touch up the pink, but unfortunately she

managed to escape! Ben and I spent the next hour and a half running around the farm trying to catch the pink sheep, but she was having none of it. She ran through Ben's grandad's garden, up into another field, down the road, went into a muddy ditch and then ended up in the field on the marsh with the cows. The cows didn't like the pink sheep and the pink sheep wouldn't come anywhere near us. By this point Ben hated the pink sheep and I was in tears. Eventually the pink sheep came to a stop but only because she got stuck upside down, on her back, in the bottom of another muddy ditch! At this point we had no choice but to wash her completely to get rid of the mud, which meant losing most of her remaining pinkness. Despite this we used the two new cans of pink hairspray that I had got and done our best to make her more of a pastel pink this time rather than neon pink. I had even rung up a couple of places in Harleston and the surrounding area to see if they had a stock of any pink hairspray, but no one did because they had been sold out because of all the Pink Ladies.

The pink sheep was left on the trimming stand for a bit just to help it dry, whilst we sorted out the Jacob sheep that we would be taking to the show. We finally got all the sheep loaded onto the trailer and put a sheep hurdle between the Jacobs and the pink sheep to make sure that the pink sheep couldn't get near the freshly washed Jacobs. Unfortunately, by the time we finally made it down to Kent and opened the trailer, the pink sheep had managed to jump over the sheep hurdle and was in with the Jacobs. Ben's sparkling white and black Jacobs now all had a pink tinge to them, which many other sheep owners found highly amusing. Ben and I then spent the next two hours washing the sheep and trying to trim out what we could. We finally started cooking dinner at 10pm and I don't think Ben's friends will let him live it down about the naughty pink sheep.

After being a pink lady every year since 2014, including the Boundary Farm breakout in 2020, I have never been prouder to be a part of such an incredible event year after year, and there really isn't anything else quite like it. Thank you Annie, John, Libby and all the behind-the-scenes pink ladies' team for everything you do to make this tractor run possible!

Sarah T

Two Vendeuvre Triumphs and One Unimog Failure!

Amid cheers, smoke and noise the Pink Ladies' Tractor Run at Harleston takes off with the only ruling that tractors are driven by women.

My Vendeuvre lent itself happily to the challenge, my husband made a breast cancer logo of steel attached to the rear which was then decorated with maximum pink balloons. Effective when moving with the occasional POP …

Because we are simply all following in single file behind leader Annie through tracks, farms and pathways I honestly could not recall the route. I missed a junction with cries of dismay from marshals but surprised them by cracking a three-point turn and catching up.

The second attempt with the Vendeuvre came off well with bedroom child's net canopy which inflated with movement. Madonna-style traffic cones painted pink enhanced the front of the tractor. I was a lady driver but a lot of hard work, organising and engineering beyond my remit. Yes, husbands were fantastic …

Third and final defeatist chance. Throughout the year I collected bras, bras and more bras. These had a pink wash through the machine. The Unimog was the chosen tractor that year, duly covered in a melody of pink bras. We did not get far … The marshals pulled us off the road as the Unimog was blocking the road, unable to move.

Giving Annie the sponsored money was always a joy!

Margaret R

The Bears

Having read about the first Pink Ladies' Road Run in the Tractor and Machinery magazine, Dave, my husband, suggested I join the 2005 Road Run. I thought he had lost his marbles because we live in Dorset about 200 miles away. Anyway, I phoned Annie and she sent me the details and 2005 was my first Road Run and it had a special meaning because my Mum's best friend for over eighty years was suffering with breast cancer.

We had an eventful journey having left home at 7.30am on the Saturday morning with the tractor loaded on my youngest son's lorry. Just after joining the M3 one of the tyres went off bang, but after Dave quickly put the spare on, we were on our way again. All went well until we took the wrong turning off the A12 and ended up going towards Newmarket. Part way along another tyre went off so I phoned the RAC who didn't want

to know because we were in a lorry. Not knowing the area I phoned Annie for help and she suggested the Keeble family at Harleston Tyres, who gallantly came to our rescue although we were miles away from Harleston. We finally arrived at the campsite in Diss, where we were staying overnight and put our tent up at about 7.30pm. I thought "never again", but I am still doing the Road Run 17 years on.

The following year Dave suggested finding a campsite near Harleston which was the start of a lovely friendship with Chris and Cherryl Thomas, and we have stayed with them each year since, and gone on lovely canal boat holidays together as well as house sitting for them over the years.

In 2011 two bears and a rabbit made an appearance on the tractor for William and Kate's wedding, when a friend of mine dressed one of the bears in full military uniform and in 2012 the rabbit was replaced by a third bear and one of the bears was Annie carrying the Olympic torch. Since then all three bears have appeared each year in various costumes but all wearing bras.

In 2015 the Road Run became even more important to me because my daughter Rachel was diagnosed with terminal stage 4 bone cancer and secondary breast cancer on 12 March just two days after her 35th birthday. She had a major operation in November 2015 to replace the fractured vertebrae in her neck with a metal plate and cage over it. In early 2016 she had the lump in her breast removed and also her lymph nodes. After one of her scans in 2018 showed she had another lump, she had a mastectomy. Luckily in March 2020 she was able to celebrate her 40th birthday the weekend before the first lockdown, which was something she thought she may not see because she was given an average life expectancy of five years. Due to having treatment every three weeks since her diagnosis she is still with us seven and a half years on and her latest scan showed that the cancer hasn't got any worse at the moment.

I was all prepared to do the Road Run this year, which would have been my 17th, but had to drop out at short notice having had to go into hospital for an operation and was unable to drive on 3 July. The operation was originally scheduled for 9 February but had to be cancelled due to me testing positive for Covid on 6 February. All being well I will be back next year with the bears.

Jacquie

My Cancer Journey

Working at the time at Onward Enterprises, December 2003, time for my routine mammogram. – I was fine! Berated some of the other ladies at work, because they said it was too painful and uncomfortable to have done, said to one of them: "It could save your life". Little did I know.

January 2004, sitting in the canteen at work, having a meeting, could hear a phone constantly going off in a locker, after the meeting checked and it was mine. A number I didn't recognise, went to put it back and it rang, answered and it was from the hospital saying they needed me to go back for another mammogram, could I go in three days' time?

Drove there, thinking I could pop into Norwich afterwards and do some shopping, convinced that the last mammogram had a flaw, which needed checking.

Took good book, not been reading long and was called in. I was shown my mammogram and the doctor pointed out a white area (meant nothing to me), she said they needed to check more thoroughly. So another mammogram; wait; needed to do an ultrasound, still no alarm bells ringing. Had the ultrasound, then the doctor came to see me and said they needed to do a deep core biopsy, very unpleasant, face down on a bed with a hole for your breast to go through, don't think I would like another one. Told to come back in a week.

Next week, my friend Barbara came with me, so we could go shopping after, I was called through, the doctor sat there with a nurse, then alarm bells finally woke up. The doctor was lovely, but after his first words *I am afraid it is cancer and a high grade, we will need to do a mastectomy*, my brain went numb (that's the only way I can describe it). The nurse called Barbara in and she asked all the necessary questions. My first words: *I don't want to lose my nipple* – crazy, I know. The nurse said the cancer was very near the nipple so it would have been impossible to keep it, even if they could have done a lumpectomy. Next step to see the plastic surgeon to discuss reconstruction. Miss Sassoon, the most wonderful lady I ever met. Very down to earth, liked her as soon as I met her, trusted her. As I am big breasted, she said, "Well there's no way I can get near the size of the other one, what about a reduction of the other at the same time?" Of course I said no. I told them I needed time to get my head round this, to be ready, couldn't just come in and do it. They understood but said no longer than two weeks.

Monday 9 February 2004, hospital at 7am. Everything packed, lovely wrapped present from my boss's wife. Had included everything like wipes, a fan, cream, ex-nurse she knew exactly what I needed, kind thought. Had all tests, blood pressure, E.C.G. Tried to read, walked around the ward, Miss Sassoon came to see me at 9pm and drew over my breast and tummy with black felt tip. She was using the fat from my stomach. Clever.

Not a good night's sleep. Awake early, taken down at 8am, when I woke up I looked down, saw the dressing, but my breast had gone, nothing there. Very upset. Miss Sassoon came in and explained that I had small veins, so not possible to operate, they tied some off to make them swell and had to wait a week on the ward for the reconstruction.

On the second day after the operation I was very down, couldn't understand it as I knew it would eventually be done, my cancer nurse, Chris, came down and explained this was very normal, always the second or third day this happened.

The day for the reconstruction arrived. Awake early, eager to get this over. After the operation, I took a while to come around as my blood pressure had dropped, they told me. But Miss Sassoon said all had gone well. Woke up with drips in, but so pleased it had at last been accomplished. It was late at night, I needed the toilet, pressed the buzzer, bed pan in place, could I go? NO! Apologised to the night nurse, lay down, but still needed to go. Again bed pan and again my bowels would just not let go. Happened four times, then the nurse came in and put a tube there, as soon as it was attached to the bag I filled it – oh, the relief!

On the fourth day, the breast was very itchy, and parts of it had gone black. Miss Sassoon came and looked and I asked her what would happen if it went all round. She said, "Oh, we will just cut it off!" My horrified look made her laugh. Was used to her sense of humour then.

I was in hospital for three weeks, various difficulties, back home, felt very strange, but soon back to normal life.

But on Monday 12 April, I woke to a very hot and red breast, and felt very poorly. Phone my cancer nurse and she said come in. A good friend, Jane, took me, so glad she did, they took my temperature and said it was an infection, back to the same ward. Nurses joked *what are you doing back* and *know you love us but* … I was so poorly that from the Thursday it was family visiting only. Temperature continued to rise. On Saturday 17 the nurse took my temperature that night, knew by his face it was bad, told him, "I really don't feel well." He called a young doctor down who said this had gone on long enough. Had been on an antibiotic drip since I had come in, but wasn't working. He decided to put me on an antibiotic for the flesh-eating bug but I said it would blow the veins in my hand. Had been with cannulas all week, which had blown the veins, had them in my neck, ankle, hand, all over the place. But the drip worked. Woke the next morning to a really vile smell and when I looked down there was green gunge everywhere. Another operation, lost some of the breast, but felt so much better. Trips to outpatients to have the abscess cleaned from the inside twice a week. Last appointment 12 May, took nurses flowers, chocolates, etc. Had got to know them all well. Walked into outpatients and they said, "You're booked in."

I have just had another cancer scare. Found a lump near the nipple on my good breast, doctors straight away, referred urgently. Back to the hospital, mammogram, ultrasound. Very thorough, showed me the screen as she was doing it. NOT CANCER! Celebrated at home with a mountain of chocolate.

Carol

Behind the CREAKY Door

I believe I heard someone coming. The door creaks and groans as it lets in some daylight. Yes, here comes someone, I hope I am being taken out for a run, it does seem ages since I was taken for a drive, expect they will wash me down with cold water first - brrrr. But it looks like a nice warm day. They try to start my engine but I've been sitting here not going anywhere for a year so I am not ready to go yet. It seems like I have a problem with my spark plugs, damp or dirty I hear them muttering. Away they go with them to repair or replace, maybe tomorrow I will go for a run.

Next afternoon the creaky door opens again, the plugs are fitted, fuel checked and gear engaged, my engine is running. Now to the wash bay and with last year's dust removed I am ready to be taken on a run. My lady driver appears on the scene and takes me out for a spin round the country lanes. Wow, it's good to be out and about again. In a couple of days I shall be joining up with many other tractors to complete the Pink Ladies' tractor run.

Next day I am decorated from bonnet to tyres with pink bows, balloons, fluffy toys, flowers and the breast cancer logo. I stand patiently whilst my grey body is transformed into a wonderful pink vision.

Standing back in the barn waiting for the big day tomorrow, feeling very excited and remembering the many times I have been out on this special run.

The special day is here and off I go with my lady driver all dressed in pink. We make our way to Thorpe Abbotts airfield to meet up for the start of the run with over 100 of my tractor friends. They arrived in many shapes and sizes, some being driven, others carried on lorries and trailers, but all wonderfully dressed in pink. I am wondering who I will follow today. As we are shown to our starting place I realise that I shall be following another Grey Fergie and close behind me will be a large tractor, better behave myself or I could get in trouble.

Lots of people come and look with interest at all the tractors while I wait to leave and my driver is registering us.

My driver is back in the seat, others are leaving. We join the procession and we gently weave our way around country lanes and we are cheered by crowds of supporters along the route. Harleston is an amazing sight, so many people the paths were four deep, all clapping and cheering us all on our way. Shop fronts had all been decorated in pink and pink tractor flags were flying in the sunshine ...

Eventually we reach a nice peaceful meadow at Gawdy Hall where I am refuelled and rested while my lady driver joins her family for a well-deserved picnic. After the rest we are on the move again; leaving the hard tarmac behind we are now travelling across fields. It is a bit bumpy, but I am an old hand at that, reminds me of my time on the farm years ago when I was used to help plough and pull trailers. Oh, now we are back on tarmac, no more dreaming. Making our way back to Thorpe Abbotts, still crowds along the way, many at Pulham St Mary and Rushall. We arrive back at the airfield, it was a good run today and I am proud to have helped raise some money for such a really special cause.

Soon be back in the barn again as we are now on our journey home after a very successful day, cars hoot at us on the way. The farm is in sight. Home, and I am backed into the barn and the creaky door closes. My pink will disappear tomorrow then I will have to wait till next year before I can have a run out again.

Audrey

Mum

When my Mum was diagnosed with breast cancer, she showed my sister and I (both teenagers at the time) the lump in her breast. Got us to prod it and poke it, so that we knew what a tumour might feel like, so that we might have a better chance of recognising this awful thing if it ever visits one of us. I had some schoolfriends over and she invited them to come and have a poke too. They did. More girls armed with potentially life-saving knowledge.

The day before her mastectomy, we threw Mum a tea party. My sister made a boob cake, pink and round with a nipple on top made of icing. Mum cut the cake with a great big knife. We all needed a laugh.

My Mum was clever – I mean really, startlingly clever. And funny. She had a way of disarming people and making them feel comfortable, and then getting into a really good conversation with them. It meant a lot to people to be asked what they thought, and to feel heard. When she was recovering from chemotherapy, our house filled up with her PhD students who came to cook, to clean, to chat.

She was in remission for a year or two. Long enough for us all to start relaxing a bit. Not long enough.

I miss her every day. I miss her when I hug my children, and when I hear myself saying phrases that she used to say to me as a child. Words I'd held within myself all this time, dormant for so many years, and activated now that I have my own little ones. *Be kind to yourself* (great advice*); I try so hard* (said defeatedly when one of the kids really pushes my buttons – I get it now, Mum).

I wish she had been in my life for longer. 2023 will mark a strange sort of turning point for me; the moment will come when I have lived more years of my life without my Mum than the years I had with her. But when I hear my mother's words coming out of my own mouth, it makes me feel like she has been with me all this time. She is part of me, built into my foundations. And although we didn't have enough time, the time we had was rich.

Ania

David Brown

The name which I carry is proud David Brown
I am known as a worker, of strength and renown
I have ploughed and have harrowed, I have sprayed and have sown
For years they have valued the crops I have grown

But now I'm retired, I'm allowed to be lazy
Until the day that they all went quite crazy
God knows what possessed them, I just cannot think
To cover my best bits with glittering pink

I once took great pride in the title: Cropmaster!
But now, dressed in pink, it was all a disaster
Then I looked, and I shrieked, "You have all gone too far
You have draped on my nose a massive pink bra!"

But having no choice, I swallowed my pride
And I took a young lady along for the ride
And then Harleston, oh Harleston, emotional place
Gave a leap to my heart, put a grin on my face

I'll put up with the pink, and the flowers (which stink!)
I'll wear ribbons and bows and whatever you think
Will make people turn out to clap and to cheer
As long as you'll promise to take me next year!

Anon

Perseverence

It was 2007 when Annie asked me to take part in the Pink Ladies' Tractor Road Run for Cancer Research. I had never driven a tractor before so it was a bit daunting, but I wanted to take part for this very good cause.

I was lucky enough to be offered a Massey Ferguson 135 by owner Denis, I loved this tractor. For the next five years I drove it, but unfortunately in 2012 Denis sold the tractor.

The next year 2013 I was offered an International Harvester B276 by owner Graham. I have driven this tractor now for ten years.

In 2009 I had an appointment to have a scheduled mammogram in a mobile unit in Harleston. Unfortunately, the appointment was cancelled because of a breakdown. Another appointment was made for a few weeks later but this appointment was also cancelled. I persevered, and made another appointment, and fortunately this appointment went ahead.

The scan showed that I had a very small low grade lump, so small that not even the doctor could feel anything. I was admitted to hospital and the lump was removed, fortunately no chemo was necessary, only radiography and Tamoxifen for five years, when I was told then that I was all clear. After the second cancellation had I given up and left it for another three years, things could have been very different.

I am very glad I persevered!

Helen

Tractors ....

There's a pink one,
There's a blue one,
There's a big one,
There's a diddy one,
They all meet up on the airfield,
In the sunshine or the rain,
They're all dressed up in their finery,
Some of them drive,
Like they're from a winery,
There are smiles from all that see them,
As they rumble along the way.

Then there's the ladies,
In their costumes,
Some are humorous
And some are wonderful,
But the message,
They keep on sending,
Every year is just the same,
They'll tug your heartstrings,
Then your tears bring,
But most of all,
They'll make you our song sing,
As they travel through the countryside,
Up and down the roads and lanes.

Lining streets,
In towns and villages,
There's people waving,
And people cheering,
Digging deep,
Into their pockets,
To support,
The tractor train,
Tears are flowing,
Through all the smiling,

At Gawdy Hall,
They'll be arriving,
For a picnic and an ice cream,
As they celebrate the day,
People sit talking,
People are walking,
Some look at tractors,
While some are maudlin,
Thinking of friends, thinking of relatives,
That have been lost,
Before today.

Just you remember,
Don't let it offend ya,
To this disease,
We'll never surrender,
Because one day,
Some time in the future,
It'll be beaten,
That's the prayer we say.

So Pink Ladies 'n' Annie Chapman,
And all the people,
Who help make it happen,
Thanks a million,
Thanks a squillion,
For a really special day ...

Peter

All In Pink

When I had the conversation with Annie that she was planning a sponsored Pink Ladies' Tractor Run I was in remission from cancer myself, so this was very dear to my heart.

I offered to organise ladies dressed in pink to carry buckets to collect monies from all the people coming to look. I think at the start there were about 3 of us, but last year there were 16 ladies, all dressed in pink, from the first house at Shotford Road in Harleston, right through the town, to the last estate as you left Harleston at Redenhall Road – the entire Tractor run route through the town. We were not going to miss anyone! The ladies work in pairs and have their own 'territory' and it is hilarious if anyone else goes on their patch, all done in good humor and makes the crowd smile. And the crowds – wow! There are more and more people every year, one year I asked in our Harleston Grapevine magazine for anyone watching to wear pink – and they certainly did. All added to the wonderful atmosphere of clapping and cheering as the Ladies go through. We also have ladies with buckets in the villages the tractors go through.

I also have ladies making pink bunting which either hangs outside the shops or in the windows , and we have large flags, which hang above business premises for a week before and usually a week after to remind the community to donate, the flags include Annie's tractor. A real social event for the town, as well as so very important for all the money raised in that hour/ hour and a half.

Carol

My Pink Ladies' Tractor Runs

Having watched the tractors leave and return from the early runs I had the opportunity to have a tractor from a local farm, a Massey Ferguson, which I took, and it was an amazing day, a real eye opening: people out in gardens, field gateways and lining both sides of the road in Harleston on our way to lunch at Gawdy Hall. Wow, Harleston is very supportive of the tractor run!

My next drive I had a David Brown which I drove for five very enjoyable years, then the tractor was sold. I went a few years without a tractor to drive, I still watched and donated, but in 2022 talking to a friend I was then able to acquire a tractor again from someone who had lost his wife to breast cancer, this time it was a John Deere. I joined a group of six ladies of which three generations of one family taking part, the mum having done all the runs from the start. Hearing four friends from the village all being diagnosed with breast cancer in early 2022 made it more important to take part again, it's only January and just heard another school friend has just been diagnosed with it.

Tractor sorted, decorations sorted and hopefully cross the million pound line this year.

Lilian

Worth Doing!

The first time I sat on a tractor was at Thelnetham Windmill open day and it was a Fordson Dexta! It fitted me just fine. SOOO the next thing was to look for a Dexta of my own, luckily my husband knew exactly where there was a scrapped one.

Then it all started with a phone call from Annie one evening suggesting the ladies' tractor run. I remember counting up to about 10 on my fingers so I thought "Yeah this would be worth doing", Annie got into gear and put the word about and as they say the rest is history.

So July 2004 the pink ladies were born and started raising money for Breast Cancer charity, we had 50 participants starting from South Green, Pulham St Mary, me included we made our way through the lovely Waveney valley to Sylham Hall for our pink picnic lunch and then on to Harleston and back. Now that there is over 100 tractors so thankfully we are really lucky now to start from Thorpe Abbots Airfield which has plenty of space for us all to unload, decorate and parking for all our families that come to support us, as some have a long way to come!

So far I have participated in every road run and m daughter Jo joined us after the first two. Last year i 2022 my 19 year old granddaughter Ebony also too part for the first time, she was a bit nervous to begi with but it all went really well and she's also hooked.

We all enjoy going through Harleston, it is s emotional seeing our flags flying and people callin out and waving, shortly after this we now have ou lunch at Gawdy Hall where all our family and friend gather together. After lunch we hit the road again fo our homebound journey and this time, we do quite bit of off road around the headlands. Jono is usuall found along the route armed with his camera catchin really good photographs of us all, from here we ar now heading towards Pulham St Mary where we ge a large applause from the crowd that gathers outsid Pennoyers. Before we know it we are now back at th Airfield for our group photograph. Even though th run is over, the fundraising efforts continue with ladie organising all sorts of events throughout the year. W all look forward to September when we attend ou cheque presentation night at Annie's.

Pam

Family Affair

It's a real family affair for us all, as amazingly my mum has done every run so far and I only missed the first two due to having a young daughter who this year joined us on her first run. The pink ladies and Annie hold a very special place in our family's hearts, and it's made it even more emotional this year having had three generations taking part beside each other

There's such a buzz around the whole event and the support we get when fundraising is phenomenal. My family and my friend Jayne always love arranging charity events like quizzes, bingo nights and dog shows, and we are so lucky with what people are willing to give and how they support us with donations that makes it a lot easier for us to contribute to our ever growing total!

Dad has been asked on a few occasions to transport a bride to church on her wedding day by tractor and trailer with the payment just a donation to the pink ladies!

We always look forward to the day of decorating when our whole gang congregates on mum and dad's drive, there's plenty of tea and chat flowing and then always a manic rush to get the pink paraphernalia secured safely on our tractors.

On the day of the tractor run there's usually a surprise with the weather and it rarely ends how it starts, so plenty of changes or sun cream throughout the day! Being prepared is key, one year I wasn't and I ended up wearing dad's wax jacket, partner's waterproof golf trousers with a neon pink tutu. Sunburnt, windswept or drenched, but we don't care, as the reason behind the day is far more important! One more thing that is always guaranteed is there'll be tears driving through Harleston, where the crowd-lined Thoroughfare is just the best feeling ever!

Joanne

Breathtaking

Breathtaking. One of many ways to describe the feeling of driving your pink tractor through the country roads being supported by so many, for such a good cause. I feel extremely lucky to be a part of this event since I was born. My nan was one of the first ladies to be involved with the run after Annie came up with the crazy idea, and soon after my mum joined. So in 2022 I took part in my first run as I turned 18, having our 3 generations there together.

Since I was young, I'd been helping my mum organize her events, gathering sponsorship and marshalling the roads with my grandad. But being sat in front of the wheel this year, is a different experience. Driving through Harleston and seeing the bunting and all the smiling faces is honestly the most overwhelming feeling and can get very emotional at times.

The run isn't just a group of ladies on their tractors in Norfolk. It's a lot more than that, especially behind the scenes. As soon as we get home off the tractors, we are thinking of next year! The events we can put on to raise money, finding more decorations, sponsorship etc.

Particularly for the 2023 run where, I have no doubts we will hit our £1m target. This is a group that I am so proud to be a part of, and I just love to share the stories with people I meet. And I don't think a minute goes by where we forget the reason we take part.

Annie has played a key role in my life and is somebody I will always look up to. When asked "who inspires you", Annie Chapman is always the first person to mind and always will be my answer. Its amazing what one person has brought to so many, and what a group of ladies can bring together.

It's one day of the year for us, that affects the lives of so many.

Ebony

Marshal

I was really pleased when Annie decided to start the pink run for cancer as it gave us a chance to get our tractors out for the ladies!

I've marshalled at all the runs to date, Roger always puts me on the Brockdish junction where the water splash is and I'm always with my gang Francis, Robin and my son in law Marcus always had my granddaughter Ebony with me until last year when she took part for the first time and it was great to see her on the route alongside my daughter Jo and wife Pam.

I've even been known to take a bride or two to their weddings by tractor and trailer for a donation to the pink ladies! I just love being part of it!

To finish sadly I must mention our good friend Peter Seaman RIP who used to also marshal with us, he absolutely loved the run and it used to be the highlight of his year to see the ladies on his three tractors that he lent out for the run.

John

Inflatable Flamingos

In 2017 I witnessed a sight that stopped me in my tracks.

There I was, cycling on the backroads of South Norfolk when out of nowhere a host of women came hurtling towards me on an array of tractors bedecked in pink.

It was the vivid and widely-loved Pink Ladies' Tractor Road Run. I'd heard about it but I had never seen it in person…it was beautiful, emotional and inspiring all at the same time.

The train of tractors, from vintage machines to new models with full power steering, wound its way on a 20-mile route across the district throughout the day. Tractors were decked out in pink garlands, bras, inflatable flamingos, parasols and so much more.

But what really struck me was the enthusiasm and dedication of the women involved and I knew that they would all have their own personal stories to tell about their experiences of cancer.

I've wanted to take part since that first glimpse of the run and this year (2023) is the year it will happen.

Many years ago, I interviewed Annie for the Eastern Daily Press.

I had an hour assigned and four hours later I left inspired by the force of the woman I'd met and enthused about her event. I could have talked with her for days.

Fast forward a few years and I had moved to a village only a few miles away from Annie. I made contact and offered to volunteer, writing news stories about the run to raise its profile.

Since then, Annie has tried her best to persuade me to take part in the run and I'm sure countless other women too!

Each year around 110 women from across the country take part. Many will never have driven a tractor before, but most will have been touched by breast cancer in some way.

Some have taken part since the very start and every year a flurry of new participants join the convoy and take to the roads.

It's not only the women taking part that make the event happen, it's also down to the people who lend their tractors, the land-owners, the many marshals, the collecting crew and countless others who pull together in an extraordinary team effort.

Once I had decided to take part, the idea of sourcing a tractor seemed monumental, but this is East Anglia and thanks to a superb local farmer I now have a tractor, and although I've driven it a few times, I need more training ahead of the big day.

Then will come the enormous task of sourcing pink decorations for myself and the tractor.

As a spectator for many years, I have witnessed the crowd-lined routes. I've met the ladies, their friends and families at the picnic lunch which punctuates the route.

I've heard their inspiring and heart-breaking stories.

I've seen people along the route dressed in head-to-toe pink, cheering, clapping and crying in support – in towns, villages, laybys and gardens.

I've seen the houses and businesses bedecked in pink bunting, banners and flags.

I've witnessed it all first-hand but being part of the run and driving through the waves of support will be something else entirely.

The run does so much more than raise vital funds, it creates a support network for so many, it brings light and laughter to people at times when there may be little, it raises awareness and just maybe, it makes women check their breasts for anything out of the ordinary.

It certainly did make me check mine. Because of the run I do make those regular checks. I remember one year cycling home from the run to write about it and as I sat at my computer, I checked my breasts and found a lump. It was terrifying but thankfully turned out to be a fatty cyst.

I will be taking part in the run, thinking about the strength of the hundreds of participants that have taken part over the years and my treasured Aunty Betty who died of breast cancer.

But, I will be doing it with a huge smile on my face, hoping not to hold the convoy up or stall the tractor!

Kate

Photo opportunity

My experience of the Pink Ladies' Tractor Run

I had heard about the Pink Ladies' Tractor Run and the fantastic amount of money already raised for cancer research for many years from my good friend Robert White. I always had hopes to get over from Lincolnshire to witness it myself but there always seemed to be something get in the way. Eventually in 2021 I made the journey over to Thorpe Abbotts airfield on the morning of the run and was blown away by the sea of pink that greeted me. Even though I knew how many tractors were expected, seeing them all lined up and decked out was beyond my imagination. Not only were the tractors dressed in all shades of pink, so were most of the people.

Walking along the rows of tractors and seeing so many happy faces was a real tonic after the 18 months we'd just gone through with the pandemic. I took many photos but soon decided this was not the best way to capture them with so many people amongst them, soaking up the atmosphere and preparing the tractors for the run.

As the start time neared I made my way to the exit gate where I could photograph every one as they left. This gave me around 120 delightful pictures of the beautifully, sometimes manically, decorated tractors.

Having waved the last tractor and support vehicles off I headed to Gawdy Hall to await their arrival. Another wonderful experience was had watching the ladies expertly park their tractors in neat rows. This gave everyone another chance to walk around and admire the magnificent tractors and decorations.

I joined some of the support crew for a picnic lunch. They talked enthusiastically about how emotional the ride through Harleston had been, with supporters lining both sides of the street cheering them on.

Another fantastic photo opportunity arose as the tractors left Gawdy Hall, giving a beautiful backdrop of Norfolk grazing land, after which it was back to Thorpe Abbotts for their arrival at the final destination. It was a joy to see so many relieved ladies happy to have completed the course successfully. Within minutes tractors were being loaded on to low loaders or driven away as the successful day drew to a close. I was told that there was usually a group photo taken at this point but owing to some Covid restrictions still being in place this wouldn't happen this year.

The day was rounded off with a few of us returning to Gawdy Hall to litter pick. As could be expected with such a respectful gathering there was very little to do except pick up the occasional wrapper that had blown away rather than discarded intentionally. As I drove home reflecting on a wonderful day I knew for certain I would be back in 2022 and resolved to see the tractors parade through Harleston.

July 2022

Once again I drove over to Thorpe Abbotts for the Pink Ladies' Tractor Run on the Sunday morning. Having

a bit more idea of what to expect I made the decision to immerse myself in the occasion rather than view it through the lens of a camera. Within a few minutes of being there I found myself helping with binding brakes on a Ford Dexta. Being nearly 30 years since I worked with tractors the memories of agricultural college came flooding back, unfortunately not which way to turn the adjuster screw. Help was at hand from the partner of the lady on the next tractor and the Dexta brakes were soon running freely.

Having watched the tractors leave again I was about to head for Harleston to hopefully find a parking space somewhere near the main street. At this point my phone rang and my day was about to take an unexpected turn. Robert was calling to say that Gareth, who follows the run with Chris in his vintage Land Rover, had broken down and could I assist in any way. I found Gareth and Chris about half a mile from the start line, Gareth had called the RAC who were 'on their way'. It was decided that Gareth would stay with the Land Rover and await recovery, whilst Chris and I follow the tractors in my car to pick up the direction signs and any pink bits that fell off the tractors.

By the time we reached Harleston we weren't very far behind the tractors so I got to experience a run down the high street and witness the crowds. It truly was an emotional experience to see both sides of the street filled with cheering bystanders and the pink decorations everywhere. Amusingly, children were requesting a blast from the horn using the universal gesture of a fist pull.

As the boot of a Citroen Picasso isn't as big as a Land Rover we were beginning to wonder if we would get to Gawdy Hall before the boot was full. We did however

make it, thanks to some very skilful tessellated packing by Chris.

After a welcome picnic and ice cream at Gawdy Hall I was with Robert when he got a call to a tractor that the driver couldn't get into gear. We soon realised that modern tractors aren't our forte so Harry from Ben Burgess was called and shortly he had the gears changing with ease.

The return journey to Thorpe Abbotts went without hiccup and another successful run was this year rounded off with a group photo.

A short drive over to Gareth found him still sat with his Land Rover awaiting recovery by the RAC, so the decision was made to stand them down. Gareth was due to drive Annie's tractor back to John and Annie's, so whilst he drove the tractor, the trusty Picasso was called upon to tow the poorly Land Rover back. After safe delivery of tractor and Land Rover it was back to Gawdy Hall for a final tidy up and load all sign posts and fencing onto John's trailer.

As I headed back to Lincolnshire I once again had a lot to reflect upon from a truly wonderful day and now knew the 'lump in the throat' experience of Harleston high street during the Pink Ladies' Tractor Run.

Alan

Venice

On holiday in Venice, in 2017 I think, my wife and I were wandering along the famous waterfront, pausing here and there to have a look at the various stalls there. One of these was a news-stand, with newspapers on display, in different languages. There was a Daily Telegraph on show. I said to my wife "look, there's Harleston!" and on the front page quite a large picture of the Pink Ladies' Tractor Run passing by Barclays Bank.

Fame of the event is indeed getting round the world!

Graham

What Does the Pink Ladies Road Run Mean to Me?

In the early years of this increasingly wonderful event, I had nothing at all to do with the P.L.T.R.R. After all, why would a Man, from outside East Anglia, have any affiliation to it whatsoever?

Over the years, I gradually learned more about the event, not least from my friend Robert White, who has been tractor breakdown man/mechanic/recovery "angel" for the full 18 years the spectacle has been staged.

However, from the time my eldest son Taig (Rob's godson) joined him in the cab of his rescue tractor as "assistant mechanic", I began, gingerly, to attend the event.

My first experience of "Annie's baby" was arriving at the Gawdy Hall meadow lunch stop. Wow!! What a truly fantastic atmosphere! Within minutes I was hooked, wondering why on earth I had, in preceding years, felt it was an occasion for others – local people, not an East Midlandsonian like me!

The smell of the tractors (I am a classic tractor owner and lover myself), the sight of lunch hampers bulging with fine fare and the general, joyful ambience, made me feel I had deprived myself of several years of real fun. I could come clean and say that I don't believe I contributed financially in those early days to the HUGELY worthy cause of raising funds for Breast Cancer Research. Annie, where's your bucket?

It was not long before I adopted a role for myself on the first Sunday of July each year: that of litter picker, for the vast amounts of trash discarded by participants and their families and friends on this extremely special day. Huh! I found myself nearly out of a job on day one!

How fabulously refreshing to have to go searching for the tiniest pieces of "litter" – maybe a small piece of pink ribbon decoration detached from a tractor or a wind-blown piece of picnic cling film. If only the rest of the British population could adopt the attitude and the m.o. of the Pink Ladies and their followers ... Boy, (or should that be "Girl"?) would this country be a prettier place!

So, to the crux of the matter!

I am utterly in awe of the mind-blowing sums that Annie, John, their unwavering loyal band of assistants and of course, each and every lady participant, have raised each year. As I understand it, each lady entrant approaches potential sponsors on each year that they wish to take part in the run. For every lady who is a "regular", I can only imagine that re-approaching generous former sponsors must be a less than easy task. However, as is evidenced by the uncannily consistent high levels of revenue each year, this tells me that there are some very generous people in society. Indeed, their apparent perpetual willingness to give must be born out of their profound belief that they are supporting an exceptionally worthy cause.

With the 'Magic Million' point seemingly just on the horizon, we are approaching a very significant milestone. From a selfish viewpoint, I hope the P.L.T.R.R. continues for many more years. Alas, nobody is getting younger, so it must be recognised that advancing years put increasing mental and physical demands on the organisers. Nevertheless, I can truthfully say that I am struggling for words, sufficiently to describe my utmost admiration for Annie and what she has achieved thus far.

Charlie

Just Occasionally Help Is Needed

It has been suggested that most people know, or know of, someone who has been affected by breast cancer. On reflection I find myself no exception to this. First Granny, followed by Auntie Sue. Then a close family friend (a survivor!) and just recently her 46-year-old daughter has been diagnosed and is currently receiving treatment.

I have been involved with the Pink Ladies' Tractor Road Run for several years now. My partner Lauren has done several runs with two of my tractors: a 1994 Fendt complete with cab and air conditioning and at the other end of the scale a small International built in 1967, no cab, no creature comforts. Ask Lauren which she prefers and she will say that depends entirely on the weather on the day in question!

After much discussion with Uncle Rob, it was decided that I should join him in the cab of the breakdown recovery tractor at the rear of the convoy. From 2015 I have been an extra pair of hands available to help when needed. We would sometimes speculate as to what scenario would be our biggest challenge and concluded that a tractor broken down on Harleston High Street, blocking the road, came somewhere near the top of the list.

And so, it came to be, a few years ago: I was driving the tractor, Uncle Rob riding in the passenger seat. His phone rang, a Pink Lady was in that very situation. She thought the clutch had failed and was unable to move. To a degree, luck was on our side. This was not a 200 horse power John Deere that couldn't be budged, it was a little grey Ferguson that local bystanders (bless them) were able to push into a space next to the pavement, allowing the rest of the convoy to continue. I heard Uncle Rob gleaning as much information as he could, so by the time we arrived on scene ten minutes later, a plan between the three of us had been hatched. It seemed the Pink Lady was not panicking, and was taking the whole stressful situation very much in her stride. We were not going to be fitting a new clutch on Harleston High Street, we were going to tow that Ferguson to the Gawdy Hall lunch meadow for further investigation. It was like a well-rehearsed pit stop. I drove up and positioned myself in front of the Fergie, Uncle Rob leapt out of the cab and attached the towing

strap to both tractors, leapt back in the cab and we set off to the tremendous roar and cheers of the crowds. What a moment! We had offered for one of us to steer the Fergie (quite a strange sensation until you get used to it) while the lady rode in the towing tractor but she was having none of that. This was a very capable Pink Lady, happy, smiling and making our job so very easy. I opened the rear window of our tractor so that we could converse with her and make her feel part of the team.

Arriving at Gawdy Hall to yet more cheers and clapping we set about identifying the problem and concluded that the clutch was fine; fuel starvation was the culprit. Ideally the fuel tank needed to be removed and cleaned out and a new fuel filter fitted. Not the thing to be done at that time or place. We did manage to get the engine running again and even had time for a sandwich. What a truly beautiful place for a picnic.

When it was time to set off for Thorpe Abbots, we arranged for her to be last Pink Lady in convoy, immediately in front of us, not convinced that our quick fix would last. We were right, it didn't make it out of the meadow. So, it was hook up the towing strap once again and head for the finishing post. With our back window still open we chatted and got to know our Pink Lady quite well. It seemed the three of us were all engaged in agriculture in one way or another and a great camaraderie bonded us over those last ten miles. Back at the airfield she had completed her run, not quite as planned but a very special Pink Lady (they all are!) took her place in the group photograph with a beaming smile that said it all.

Taig

Beyond Proud

I am beyond proud to call Annie Chapman my grandmother. To me, the Tractor Run starts with her, and over the last two decades, has grown into an army that must have seemed unbelievable at the start.

At a glance, a group of 100 ladies driving vintage tractors, all dressed in pink, may seem crazy to those unknowing. An annual run of women driving around the Suffolk and Norfolk countryside, on tractors decked out in pink ribbons and bras is exactly that, crazy. But the sense of community that it brings to not just the drivers, but the supporters, the survivors, and those suffering, is infectious itself.

Having grown up with the Tractor Run around me, I've seen the growth of the Pink Ladies, which has been overwhelming, but also the loss of a few of our own. Granny Annie has explained to me that this is why we do the run, to fight against cancer, to stop it taking our Pink Ladies. Almost everyone knows someone who has cancer, and some of the Pink Ladies have had, or

have, breast cancer themselves. Aged 23, I have already seen the journey of 4 women develop and struggle with breast cancer, including my best friend's mother. All types of cancer are just relentless. Last year, I lost my other grandmother, as well as my great aunt.

Nothing that I can write even begins to explain the tidal waves of emotion of being one of the Pink Ladies. Driving through Harleston, which becomes a pink town for the day, crammed full of supporters, leaves me with a wide smile and tears all down my face.

I do the Tractor Run to raise money for Cancer Research. I also do it because it is enormous fun, because it gives me an inexplicable awareness of how precious my life is, I do it to support Granny Annie and in memory of Granny Prilly. I am so proud to be a Pink Lady, and though each of us has their own story, our goal to beat cancer remains united.

Pip

Cancer Research UK and breast cancer

The Pink Ladies' Tractor Road Run specifically supports research into breast cancer, the most common cancer in the UK[1]. Cancer Research UK's work has helped double breast cancer survival – in the 1970s, 4 in 10 women with breast cancer in the UK survived their disease for 10 years or more. Now, almost 8 in 10 women will survive their disease for at least 10 years[2].

In 2021/22, Cancer Research UK spent over £23m on breast cancer research, part of which was contributed through Annie's fundraising activity. The charity has played a part in important findings in breast cancer research, including the discovery of BRCA1 and BRCA2, genes that increase the risk of breast cancer, and the development of a number of important drugs for this disease, such as tamoxifen.

Almost 8 in every 10 breast cancers diagnosed in the UK are classified as 'oestrogen receptor-positive', or ER-positive for short. Tamoxifen is one of the most important drugs in the history of this type of breast cancer. Cancer cells in these tumours are encouraged to grow by the hormone oestrogen. But being dependent on oestrogen means it can make them sensitive to drugs like tamoxifen, which block oestrogen from affecting cancer cells. Cancer Research UK funded many large trials in the 1980s and 1990s looking at the effectiveness of tamoxifen, and its research has shaped the way the drug is used to treat breast cancer today.

The charity has also played a big role in the evolution of radiotherapy and surgery, both of which used to be harsh and invasive treatments for people with breast cancer. Radiotherapy can play an important role in preventing breast cancer coming back after surgery. In the 1990s, Cancer Research UK funded research that confirmed the benefits of radiotherapy in preventing breast cancer from returning and this led to recommendations on how to reduce side effects.

Further trials funded by the charity led to manageable and effective treatment for breast cancer, which is now the standard of care in the UK and other countries.

Surgery remains one of the most effective ways of treating cancer. For breast cancer, surgery available used to be extremely invasive, involving the removal of the entire breast and the muscles of the chest well. This surgery, known as radical mastectomies, often led to disfigurement and severe psychological impact. In 1961, Cancer Research UK looked at a new surgical technique called the lumpectomy, or breast conserving surgery. This surgery removes only the tumour and little of the surround breast tissue. The charity funded a trial that proved lumpectomies were just as effective as mastectomy for early-stage breast cancers, and importantly, had far fewer side effects. Several other studies added to this evidence and finally, in the 1990s, clinical practice changed to adopt the lumpectomy as standard of care.

Cancer Research UK's work in the breast cancer prevention space continues to this day, funding multiple trials and programmes into this specialist area. This includes research that has shown that breast cancer is not, in fact, one disease, but at least 11[3], changing forever how doctors look at the disease.

At Cancer Research UK, we're incredibly grateful to the Pink Ladies' Tractor Road Run for their support of breast cancer research. Around 55,900 people are newly diagnosed with breast cancer in the UK every year and they are the ones who will benefit most from the generosity of Annie, her participants and supporters.

1   Based on 55,900 new breast cancer cases in the UK every year (2016-2018). Cancer Research UK, www.cancerresearchuk.org/health-professional/cancer-statistics/statistics-by-cancer-type/breast-cancer#heading-Zero, Accessed February 2023.

2   Ten-year age-standardised net survival for breast cancer in women has increased from 40% for people diagnosed in 1971-1972 to a predicted survival of 78% for those diagnosed in 2010-2011 in England and Wales. Data were provided by London School of Hygiene and Tropical Medicine on request, 2014. Cancer Research UK, www.cancerresearchuk.org/health-professional/cancer-statistics/statistics-by-cancer-type/breast-cancer/survival#heading-Two, Accessed February 2023.

3   Rueda, O.M., Sammut, SJ., Seoane, J.A. et al. Dynamics of breast-cancer relapse reveal late-recurring ER-positive genomic subgroups. Nature 567, 399–404 (2019). DOI: 0.1038/s41586-019-1007-8

Fundraising support

Annie independently organises the annual tractor run in aid of Cancer Research UK. There is no formal fundraising committee, however Annie is supported by members of her local community, friends and family who all pitch in to assist her in compiling fundraising packs, promotion and carrying out event-related activity. Her husband, John, and daughter Libby Searle, both deserve a special mention for their amazing support – events like these really do take a village to be successful!

In return, Cancer Research UK provides fundraising support to help maximise the success of the event. From resources to advice to showing the impact of the fundraising on our research, we have been with Annie every step of the way. We hugely value supporters like Annie and want them to succeed – and we also like to get involved! Such is Annie's magnetism and infectious passion that some Cancer Research UK staff members – including Deborah Adams, Nicola Stapleton and Louise Cook – have all learned how to

drive a tractor so that they too can take part and show their support for the event.

One of the highlights in the Cancer Research UK fundraising calendar is the after-event activity, when Annie opens the doors to her barn and invites everyone to join her for a celebration. Staff from Cancer Research UK get to meet all the wonderful supporters and tractor drivers, while also having the opportunity to say a huge thank you to Annie.

In recognition of all that she has done, we recently nominated Annie for the Pride of Britain 'Fundraiser of the Year 2022' Award. Annie was shortlisted and appeared on ITV1 representing the East Anglian region. She was also nominated for the charity's Flame of Hope award for her charitable work over the years – and, in 2008, was awarded Volunteer of the Year. Thank you, Annie, for all that you do.

Trudy Stamer

Head of Supporter Led Fundraising
and Engagement